C000018618

Easy to read but hard to forget, *Wh* [...]
hard questions with rigour and hun [...]
watching the relentless tide of God [...]
the sandcastles of our human defences against God's claim on
our lives.
*Dave Bookless, Director of Theology for A Rocha International and
author of* Planetwise *and* God Doesn't Do Waste

I fear that sometimes the objections people raise to excuse their
non-belief in Christianity are a ruse for their unwillingness to
renounce selfish living, and follow Jesus. Michael Ots calls their
bluff. He is easy to read, relevant, enthusiastic and dares to
confront common prejudices. I would challenge all non-believers
to consider what he says.
Roger Carswell, Evangelist

What Kind of God? tackles ten thorny questions about God with
great simplicity and warmth. A good start for those who want
to investigate Christianity.
Richard Cunningham, Director UCCF The Christian Unions

What Kind of God? is a well-written, current, honest and practical
resource for those exploring the Christian faith and also for
Christians aiming to respond to questions and objections.
Michael skilfully reveals the beauty and uniqueness of Jesus
Christ in a clear and engaging way. I would give this book to
my friends.
*Sharon Dirckx, Apologist, Oxford Centre for Christian Apologetics,
and author of* Why? Looking at God, Evil and Personal Suffering

If you've ever asked tough questions about whether God is
really good – or wondered how to help someone else who does
– then you need to read this book. Michael Ots deals with the
hard issues, such as why God doesn't end suffering, why he
places limits on sexuality, or why he sends people to hell, in
a compassionate and very readable way.
  A great defence of Christianity as public truth from a brilliant
young communicator.
Marcus Honeysett, Author; Director of Living Leadership

What Kind of God? helped to equip me with the answers I needed to many of the challenges I faced at a difficult time. I would recommend this book to anyone who believes and to anyone seeking to understand more of the big questions concerning God and the Christian faith in everyday life.
Amy Kimmond, reader

Raging godlessness loses its battle here, for this book offers living water from the spring. It offers a cure. Drink of it freely.
Branislav Lecic, Serbian actor and politician

Michael has proven to be a real hit with students the length and breadth of the country with his relevant, honest and accessible answers about his faith. *What Kind of God?* is no different! Without a doubt, I'd pass *What Kind of God?* to any Christian or seeking student to help them on their spiritual journey.
Linda Marshall, UCCF Midlands Team Leader

Michael Ots approaches such burning topics as global warming, sex and suffering in relation to the God of the Bible in a warm, honest and humorous way. When it comes to knowing God, I'm sure you'll find this a deeply beckoning book.
Rico Tice, All Souls Church & Christianity Explored

WHAT KIND OF GOD?

MICHAEL OTS

WHAT KIND OF GOD

Responses to 10 popular accusations

?

INTER-VARSITY PRESS
36 Causton Street, London SW1P 4ST, England
Email: ivp@ivpbooks.com
Website: www.ivpbooks.com

First published 2008
Reprinted 2008, 2009
with new cover and updated text 2016

British Library Cataloguing in Publication Data
A catalogue record for this book is available from the British Library.

ISBN: 978-1-78359-410-8

Set in Monotype Dante 12/15pt
Typeset by CRB Associates, Potterhanworth, Lincolnshire
Printed and bound in Great Britain by Ashford Colour Press Ltd, Gosport,
Hampshire

*Inter-Varsity Press publishes Christian books that are true to the Bible and that
communicate the gospel, develop discipleship and strengthen the church for its mission
in the world.*

*IVP originated within the Inter-Varsity Fellowship, now the Universities and Colleges
Christian Fellowship, a student movement connecting Christian Unions in universities
and colleges throughout Great Britain, and a member movement of the International
Fellowship of Evangelical Students. Website: www.uccf.org.uk. That historic association
is maintained, and all senior IVP staff and committee members subscribe to the UCCF
Basis of Faith.*

CONTENTS

ACKNOWLEDGMENTS

I am so thankful to those who have invested in my life and helped me to see that God is good. Thanks to Mum and Dad, for being so faithful in your love and support. Thanks to Tim and the youth leaders at Knighton Evangelical Free Church in Leicester, for loving me, teaching me the Bible and answering my questions. Thanks, Tom, for your talk at the youth club that was to change my life for ever and for your continued friendship since.

I am deeply grateful to Peter Dray and Stanton for the hours of phone calls as we have talked through each chapter and you have given me ideas. This book would not be here if it were not for you. Thanks also to others who have given input and read through various chapters: Kath, Sandra, Max, Marcus, Malcolm and Linda. Thank you, too, to the many University Christian Unions that I have had the joy of working with, giving many of these chapters as talks.

I have also benefited greatly from listening to people like Roger Carswell and Rico Tice. Thanks also to Tim Keller, whom I have never met, but whose sermons have impacted my thinking in so many areas.

David and Sue Pickard have been a continual encouragement. Thanks so much for your hospitality as I have been writing. Thanks to all at Lansdowne Baptist Church in Bournemouth. I am so grateful to God for having had the privilege of being a part of such a warm and supportive church family. Thanks to Eleanor Trotter at IVP for keeping me to task and getting this book to where it is now. Finally, thank you to everyone else for your input into this book and into my life.

Michael Ots
June 2008

INTRODUCTION

'The God of the Old Testament is arguably the most unpleasant character in all of fiction: jealous and proud of it; a
petty, unjust, unforgiving control-freak; a vindictive, blood-
thirsty ethnic cleanser; a misogynistic, homophobic, racist,
infanticidal, genocidal, filicidal, pestilential, megalomaniacal,
sadomasochistic, capriciously malevolent bully.'[1] So begins
Richard Dawkins, in a public reading of his book *The God
Delusion*. The listening crowd cheers and applauds.

'The concept of an omniscient God has profoundly
damaged humanity . . . The world might be a great deal better
off without "him".'[2] So says the blurb of another book on the
subject. The accusations are not so much to do with whether
God exists, but with what kind of God he is. Frank Zappa
put it this way in his song 'Dumb All Over': 'Hey, let's get
serious . . . God knows what he's doin' . . . He wrote this book
here . . . An' the book says: "He made us all to be just like
Him," so . . . If we're dumb . . . Then God is dumb . . . (An'
maybe even a little ugly on the side).'[3]

I spend a large part of my time on university campuses, explaining the message of the Bible and answering questions. What I have discovered over the last couple of years is that most of the questions I get asked are about God himself. The issue is not so much God's existence as his character. How can God be good, when he authorizes war, allows suffering, represses sexuality, punishes his own Son and excludes people on the basis of their beliefs, condemning them to hell? What kind of God would be represented by hypocritical churches and fundamentalist movements? Why does he allow the environment to be ruined? How can such an old-fashioned concept have any relevance to me today?

Whoever we are, these questions are of massive importance. The question of God's goodness is not just an intellectual one. It is also deeply emotional. The conclusion we come to will have a massive impact on every area of our life. If God is not good, then even if he does exist we wouldn't want to trust him. However, if he is good, then it will change the way we think about not only him, but ourselves as well.

As a Christian, I find these questions deeply challenging. The kind of God portrayed by Dawkins is very different from the one I had come to believe and trust in as a young lad growing up in Leicester, England. I had come to the conclusion that God was good and that he loved not only the whole world, but also me personally. I was convinced that he was totally just and completely trustworthy.

However, it didn't take me long to realize that not everyone thought the same. As a teenager in an all boys' school, I discovered there were plenty of people who found the concept of God both ridiculous and repressive. I had a choice to make. I could ignore the accusations and go on believing in spite of them. Alternatively, I could face up to the questions and think them through: were they valid?

In the end, I chose the latter. If Christianity is public truth and not just a personal belief, then it has to stand up to reasoned questioning and discussion. So I and the other two Christians in the school organized 'Grill a Christian': a question time during a lunch break, where people could come and ask any questions they liked about God. To help us out, we asked a member of our local church to come and answer the questions.

In the build-up to this event we plastered the school with posters, and on the day it seemed everyone was talking about it. We arrived at the room to discover that it was already full. Mayhem was breaking out. Bananas and half-eaten sandwiches were flying across the classroom, while some pupils were smoking out of the back window. I was nervous. I couldn't see how a farmer from a local church would be able to cope with the questions of 60 angry students.

Whether or not the next hour had any long-term impact on anyone else, I don't know. However, the impression it made on me was deep. As I listened to the questions being answered, simply and sensitively, a realization dawned. What I had always believed to be true was true. It stood up to questioning. There were answers to the accusations and they sounded good.

Ever since that lunchtime event, I have sought to adopt the same attitude when I am being asked questions. I want to think them through honestly and seek to answer them as best I can from the Bible. I have tried to do just that in these pages. Obviously, the answers are not an exhaustive treatment of their subjects (so I hope they won't be exhausting, either). However, I have added a list of further reading, in case you want to look into any of the questions in more detail.

Where to start . . .

It's up to you to decide where you want to start reading this book. There may be one particular chapter that interests you especially. Well, feel free to start with that one; and then after that, whichever ones intrigue you most. (Occasionally some themes are repeated, as they are relevant to the subject being dealt with.) You don't have to read every chapter, but it would be a good idea to make sure you read the last one before you finish. Of course, you could just read it all in the conventional way, starting at the beginning and finishing at the end. I don't really mind how you do it; but please do read it!

1. DISTANT, UNINTERESTED AND SILENT?

What kind of God doesn't make himself clearer?

Legend has it that the philosopher Bertrand Russell was once asked how he would explain to God (if he discovered in the end that he actually existed) why it was that he did not believe in him. He replied, 'I would look him in the eye and say, "Not enough evidence."'

When it comes to finding God, are we left with nothing better than a cosmic game of hide and seek? Why hasn't God revealed himself more clearly? Surely he could make it all more obvious by appearing visibly, or speaking audibly?

Richard Dawkins states: 'God's existence or non-existence is a scientific fact about the universe, discoverable in principle if not in practice. If he existed and chose to reveal it, God himself could clinch the argument, noisily and unequivocally, in his favour.'[1] His unsurprising conclusion is that he believes that God almost certainly does not exist. He goes on to admit that you cannot prove someone's non-existence, in the same way as you cannot prove that there aren't fairies at the bottom of the garden. Or, as Russell puts it, just because you cannot prove that there isn't a china teapot going round the sun in an elliptical orbit, its existence is not therefore any more likely.

Is the only answer that there is no answer?

Whatever our view, is it possible to know anything about God's existence with any degree of certainty? I was sitting by the beach reading a book on this subject when an elderly man came up and sat next to me. He took one look at the book and said thoughtfully, 'I only know that I do not know.' Scepticism like that might sound very intellectual, but is it the best we can hope for? Is the only answer that there is no answer?

A friend of mine told me about when he first moved into a hall of residence at university. He soon got to know many of the other students in his hall. However, there was one student who remained a mystery. Despite knocking on the door several times, he could get no response from room D23. None of the other students had met him either. For a while they wondered whether the room was in fact empty. However, their theory was challenged when certain clues started to appear. For a start, there was the strange smell that came from under the door – probably food, though it didn't smell particularly appetizing. Then there was the strange oboe music that could be heard late at night, along with a rather peculiar dissolving sound in the sink! These didn't prove the existence of 'D23', as the mystery student had now been affectionately named by the others in his corridor, but they were very big clues that needed to be taken into account.

When it comes to the question of God's existence, there are also big clues that we need to follow.

The world around us

When it comes to the origin of life and the universe, there are four big questions that we need to ask:

- Why is there anything at all?
- Why are there living things and not just dead things?
- Why are there complex living things and not just amoebas?
- Why are these complex living things (humans) conscious thinking creatures that even bother asking this kind of question?

Now, it is popular today to suggest that evolution has completely destroyed any argument for God's existence. However, it does not answer all our questions. When it comes to the four questions above, evolution can explain only the third one.

Take the question 'Why is there anything at all?' Evolution has nothing to say on this matter. For a long time it was believed that the universe had always existed. Then scientists discovered that the universe was expanding. Extrapolating back, this meant that at some point the universe must have had a beginning: a point in time before which nothing, time and space included, existed. We may label this event The Big Bang; but what made it go bang, and why was it so big?

We are left with a universe coming about because something very powerful, that was itself outside space and time, caused it to come about. Interestingly, this fits with what the Bible says about God. He is eternal, so without cause; infinitely powerful; and outside space and time.

While the idea of an eternal God who is outside space and time is one that many find difficult to comprehend, the alternative is no less mind-boggling. Without God, you are left with nothing. Then nothing exploded to become everything.

This argument does not necessarily prove the existence of God. In fact, it wasn't originally designed to do so. Rather, it was meant to show the logical coherence of a theistic world view – a view of the world that includes a creator God. To believe in a Creator is no more incredible than to believe in the alternative.

If God is the Creator, then he is also outside of, and independent of, his creation. This means that we shouldn't reject the idea of God because we can't find him in the universe. It would be like rejecting the existence of James Dyson because we can't find him running around inside our vacuum cleaner! Christopher Hitchens claims that 'Religion has run out of justifications. Thanks to the telescope and the microscope, it no longer offers an explanation for anything important.'[2] But God is not to be found within the universe. Telescopes and microscopes won't find him. We don't find God within creation but all of it points towards him.

The Bible teaches that, in the absence of any other evidence, the creation around us would point us towards God. 'For since the creation of the world God's invisible qualities – his eternal power and divine nature – have been clearly seen, being understood from what has been made, so that men are without excuse.'[3]

> *Creation does not tell us everything about God, but it does tell us something.*

Creation does not tell us everything about God, but it does tell us something. It shows us a God of creativity, power and beauty. It is an important clue when it comes to the question of God.

Our conscience within us

Another clue is our conscience: a seemingly universal sense of right and wrong. How did we get this inbuilt mechanism for distinguishing between things that we see as good and admirable and those which are evil and despicable? When we think about subjects such as child abuse, love, murder, selflessness, envy, and compassion, it is not hard for us to categorize them as those which are good and those that aren't. Why is that? Where did morality come from? Various causes have been suggested.

Choice?

Some say that morality is simply a matter of personal choice. If we have consensus on certain issues, it is only because we all happen to have chosen the same set of values. It is certainly popular to say that we make up our own moral values, and that no one else can tell us what is right or wrong.

To the person who thinks this, I want to ask a simple question. Is there anyone in the world right now doing something that you think is wrong? Most of us would answer 'Yes'. We don't like what some people are doing: certainly not terrorists, evil dictators, or child abusers. Yet if morality is a personal choice, what right do we have to criticize what others do? What we really want is choice for ourselves, but not for anyone else. We want to reserve the right to decide upon our own values and at the same time impose them on others. If morality is just our choice, we remove the basis of being able to say that anything is ultimately right or wrong. We also know that our own standards of morality can be flawed and we don't always get it right.

General consensus?

Others may believe that we decide what is right or wrong depending on the general consensus of society. If society as a whole agrees on a set of values, then these are the ones that we should live by.

This may sound like a good explanation, but it too needs to be questioned. At one time the general consensus of British society was that slavery was acceptable; but did that make it right? In his letters from Birmingham jail, Alabama, during the civil rights movement, Martin Luther King wrote that the only way by which we can see if a human law is unjust is if we have a higher law to appeal to.

Most beneficial?

Another way by which people seek to explain morality is by arguing that we choose our values depending on what is most beneficial to us and most likely to improve our own evolutionary standing. So love and care for others will probably prove to be beneficial to us in the long run, because people will love us back and care for us too. Meanwhile, murder and hate are bad because they increase our chances of being hated and murdered ourselves.

However, being good is not always immediately beneficial. Those who protected Jews in Nazi Germany were doing good, but it was not in this sense 'beneficial' for them. If a married man discovers that his wife is unable to have children, then from an evolutionary point of view the most beneficial thing to do is to find another woman.

'Ought' and 'is'

To be able to say that things are actually right or wrong, we need more than choice, general consensus, or an understanding of what is beneficial. Ultimately, we need a standard that is bigger than ourselves and our society. We need God. Without God, we may be able to say that things *are*, but we will never be able to say whether they *ought* to be as they are, or not.

We can observe that there are such things as love, compassion, and care, as well as such things as murder, hate, rape and abuse. However, with no higher standard to appeal to, we can never truly say that some of them *ought* to be, and others *ought not* to be. As author James Sire states, 'Among modern thinkers accepting the absence of God, so far no one has found the basis to distinguish between right and wrong. I maintain that it is in principle impossible for one ever to be found. If we are to be good (really good, not just thought to be good), a God who is good will have to exist.'[4]

We may try hard to explain away the clue of our own conscience. However, it is still a strong clue in the God question. I am not saying that you have to believe in God to make moral decisions. God's existence is not dependent on my belief in him, anyway. However, without the objective reality of God, there would be no conscience.

More than just clues

However, while conscience may point us towards God's existence, it may all still sound a bit vague. Do we have more than a scientific debate and a discussion of psychology to go on? How can we know for sure?

If my friend at university had really wanted to find out about 'D23', then he would have needed more than clues. The best thing would be to meet this mystery person: for 'D23' to come out of his room and introduce himself publicly (something I don't think he ever did!). However, the staggering evidence of history is that the God of the universe has revealed himself within it.

God on planet earth

At the start of the book of John in the Bible, we read: 'In the beginning was the Word, and the Word was with God, and the Word was God.'[5] We go on to discover that this 'word' was responsible for creation and the source of all life. All very impressive. But it is what John goes on to say that is even more staggering:

> The Word became flesh and made his dwelling among us. We have seen his glory, the glory of the One and Only, who came from the Father, full of grace and truth.[6]

In this amazing verse, John claims that the God who created the world, the source and giver of life, has been revealed in history in flesh and blood. The person in question is the focus of John's book: Jesus himself. The claim of John and the other Gospel writers is that in Jesus, God has revealed himself in history, as a man. This is a massive claim to make, and hugely significant for us.

If God has revealed himself objectively and publicly in space and time, it means we can check this out for ourselves. Because John is making a claim about a person who lived and moved in history, we can objectively look at the evidence. We can see what the documents say about him and examine whether they are reliable. To discount the existence of God without seriously considering Jesus is foolish.

Yet this is exactly what Richard Dawkins does. In a book that seeks to deny the existence of God, Dawkins devotes just five pages to looking at the evidence for Jesus. He makes unsubstantiated claims and takes verses from the Gospels out of context, showing a lack of serious consideration of what they actually say. He concludes:

> Although Jesus probably existed, reputable biblical scholars
> do not in general regard the New Testament (and obviously
> not the Old Testament) as a reliable record of what actually
> happened in history, and I shall not consider the Bible further
> as any evidence for any kind of deity.[7]

However, the Bible's accounts of Jesus' life deserve far more examination than that. Using standard methods for checking the historical reliability of texts, we find that the Gospels come out far more favourably than many other texts from that time that we generally consider reliable. The sheer numbers of early copies, from so close to the original date of writing, mean that we have good reason for believing that the Gospels are indeed authentic accounts of Jesus' life written by his contemporaries. The sheer quantity of manuscript evidence means that we can know that the Bible hasn't been changed by political powers either in the fourth century or at any subsequent point in history.

Another important thing to note is the absence of any other documents from the same era that discount the claims of the Gospels. It wasn't until much later that people began to question them. At the time people couldn't do so, because even those who were not Christians could not publicly deny the events surrounding Jesus' life. These were too well known, and there were too many witnesses. It is very hard to explain the massive early growth of a faith based upon historical events if those events were known to be false.

Why so sure?

I remember chatting to a friend who was arguing passionately about evolution, and how he felt that it showed that God could not exist. Eventually, realizing that I hadn't been persuaded, he turned to me and asked, 'Why do you believe in God? Why are you so confident that you are willing to spend your life telling people about him?' It was a great question.

'It is not because I am convinced that God created the world,' I replied, 'even though I am convinced that he did. I believe, because I cannot get away from a man called Jesus: a man who made claims greater than any man has ever made; who has done things greater than any man has ever done; a man for whom I can find no reasonable explanation other than that he was who he said he was.'

What are the implications of all this, when it comes to the question of God?

Distant?
God is not distant; in fact, quite the opposite. One of Jesus' names was 'Immanuel', which means 'God with us'. Jesus shows that, rather than being distant from us, God has come near and lived among us. The Bible says that, for those who believe in him, he is still with us each moment, by his Spirit.

Uninterested?
Neither is God uninterested in this world. He is interested enough to step into it and become part of it. Throughout history, God has been involved in the world that he made.

Imagine that somewhere in the University of Aberdeen there is a group of people who don't believe that I exist. Let's call them Amichaelists. They meet each Wednesday lunchtime to discuss my non-existence and show how evidence of my existence is fabricated and false. If I wanted, I could choose to go to Aberdeen next Wednesday lunchtime and reveal myself to them. I could show them convincingly that I do indeed exist. However, while I might have saved them some time, I wouldn't really have changed or improved their lives!

When God stepped into this world in the person of Jesus, he was doing more than winning an argument or proving his existence. Rather, he came to deal with the greatest problem of our world. He was interested enough in you and me not only to come but to willingly die. The result is not only that we may know about him, but that we may know him personally.

Silent?

Through Jesus, God has spoken clearly and distinctively in history. The book of Hebrews in the Bible says, 'In the past God spoke to our forefathers through the prophets at many times and in various ways, but in these last days he has spoken to us by his Son.'[8] God has come near and spoken. I can listen to the radio anytime and anywhere; all I need to do is switch it on. In the same way, God is continually able to speak to us. If we want to listen to what Jesus has to say, then all we need to do is read one of the Gospels in the Bible. Why not get hold of one and read it for yourself?[9] If God has spoken, then surely he is worth listening to?

2. OUTDATED, OUT OF TOUCH AND OLD-FASHIONED?

What kind of God is still relevant?

It's a cold February morning. I'm standing in the middle of the university campus with other members of the Christian Union, during their special events week, a questionnaire in my hand. Some people stop and engage in long conversations. Others walk by at double speed, as if we wanted to sign them up for the Skydiving Without a Parachute Club. Someone else sees who we are and politely remarks, 'I'm not into religion,' in much the same way as they might dismiss a member of the Sci-fi Society. Another says, 'I'm too busy to think about God.'

Irrelevant?

To some, God just seems irrelevant. They may not be passionately irreligious; they just don't see why it is important to them. I guess, by the fact that you are reading this chapter, that you are probably at least a bit more interested than that. However, you may be wondering whether God is really quite as important as Christians often make out. For a start, isn't he too old-fashioned to be relevant?

Living in the past?

Western society often prides itself on its ability continually to evolve and move forward. The idea of believing something that is two thousand years old seems like a rather large step in a backward direction. Haven't we moved on from such primitive ideas? Shouldn't we know better?

Yet how much has the world changed in two thousand years? On one level, it has changed massively. The differences in technology and communication in my lifetime alone have been incredible. Merely owning a mobile phone used to be a status symbol, and a computer with 64k of RAM was once considered advanced. There have been huge changes in moral and ethical attitudes. A few years ago global warming and environmental issues were voiced only by fringe political groups. Today they are part of the mainstream.

Yet while some things have changed, others haven't. The basic needs and desires of society haven't changed that much. In Jesus' day people still grappled with the problems of war, poverty, suffering, injustice, sickness, foreign occupation and national security.

It is true that in the Bible God does not have anything to say about how to fix your computer, what car to buy, or which phone upgrade you should get. However, on the more important and deeper issues of our lives and society, the Bible has much to say.

We like to think that as a society we are making progress, advancing, improving. Yet, how do we know that we are advancing in the right direction? After all, there were many who celebrated the progress and advancements of Nazi Germany. It is a misconception to think that all change is

How do we know that we are advancing in the right direction? positive. Will *all* the progress that we celebrate today be remembered in such a positive way in fifty years' time? Why should we think that we have *all* the answers, and that all that has gone before is wrong? New is not necessarily better.

Living on a different planet?

We want to know how to fight terrorism, cut violent crime, solve the housing shortage, pay off our university debt and sort out the health service. These seem more important than singing songs and discussing ancient texts. Christians can appear to be living on a different planet: too heavenly minded to be of any earthly good. Sadly, this may be true of some Christians, for whom churchgoing is little more than a form of escapism from the harsh realities of contemporary life.

Yet in the Bible God does have a lot to say that is very relevant to our contemporary concerns, even though these may not be addressed by name. The Bible is not an A–Z handbook for sorting out the problems of our world – we can't just find 'terrorism' under 'T' and discover a simple three-step solution.

What the Bible does do is to put our issues and problems into the bigger picture of the story of the whole world. Knowing where we have come from and where we are going helps us to understand the particular issues that we face today. The specific issues that each generation faces are actually symptoms of a deeper problem running through the history of the world.

If I have a headache, I can take a paracetamol to eliminate the pain. However, this will deal only with the symptoms of what may be a far more serious illness. Through the Bible,

God helps us to understand the world in which we live and the real reason why it has gone wrong. When we understand the big picture, we will be better equipped to deal with the individual situations that we encounter.

Universally relevant

We may cringe at the old-fashioned practices of some Christians. But equally off-putting can be Christians who are trying just a little too hard to be 'cool'. In an attempt to 'make' God 'relevant' for this generation, everything has to be new. But do Christian rock concerts, internet sites and celebrities make God relevant?

The reality is that Christianity either is or is not relevant. No amount of contemporary style will make it relevant, if it is not. No amount of old-fashioned baggage will remove its relevance, if it is.

Imagine that I am on the beach in Thailand on 26 December 2004, hours before the Boxing Day tsunami hits. I set up a little stall and invite people to come to listen to a talk on plate tectonics and their effects on coastal regions. No one comes. Hardly surprising; people are on holiday, after all, and don't want a geography lesson. So what should I do? I could make the talk interactive and include a PowerPoint presentation. I could have cool backing music and offer free tea and coffee after the meeting. Yet would that succeed in attracting more people? Probably not!

If I really want to get people's attention, all I need to do is let them know there is a tsunami on the way. I don't need to make the tsunami relevant by trying to be cool. I alert people to the fact it *is* relevant, whether they like it or not.

If the claims of Jesus are true, then they have massive relevance to everyone living on planet earth. The claims are universal, whether we like it or not, or know it or not. Some people dismiss Jesus as a personal preference; a nice person to believe in, if you are that way inclined. But Jesus did not leave that option open to us. A brief look at some of his claims shows us that they are far too big to be dismissed so easily.

He claimed to be the centre point of history

Early in Jesus' public ministry he went into the Jewish synagogue in his home town. He read the words of a prophecy from a scroll:

> The Spirit of the Lord is on me, because he has anointed me to preach good news to the poor. He has sent me to proclaim freedom for the prisoners and recovery of sight for the blind, to release the oppressed, to proclaim the year of the Lord's favour.[1]

Reading scrolls in a synagogue was not unusual for any Jewish man. But what happened next was extraordinary. With everyone's eyes upon him, Jesus said simply, 'Today this scripture is fulfilled in your hearing.'[2] Slowly, the audience began to realize what Jesus was claiming: that those words had been written about *him*. He was the person the Old Testament was talking about. Soon, the crowd became furious and literally wanted to kill him.

Jesus' claim is massive. If I walked into my local church, picked up the Bible and said 'Today, in my presence, this book is fulfilled,' then the people would think I was crazy and they would be right. Jesus claimed that he was the centrepiece of history: the one who held everything together.

He claimed to speak with eternal relevance

On another occasion, Jesus was speaking to a group of religious fundamentalists. Offended at his teaching, they asked, 'Are you greater than our father Abraham? He died, and so did the prophets. Who do you think you are?'[3] Jesus' response is astonishing. Rather than back down and apologize for such presumption, he replied, 'I tell you the truth . . . before Abraham was born, I am!'[4]

The crowd didn't apathetically respond by saying, 'It's nice you think that.' Rather, they picked up stones to kill him. They realized the implications of what Jesus had said. It wasn't that he was using bad grammar. By using the words 'I am', he was applying to himself the name that God had told the Jews was his alone. He was not only claiming to have seen a man who had died two thousand years before; he was claiming to be the eternal God.

This answers the accusation that Christianity is outdated. If Jesus was just a man, it would be reasonable to expect that the things he said have little relevance to us today. However, if he is eternal, then the things he said were not just the product of his time but come with eternal relevance, from the eternal God. Many of his stories may have been about first-century farming, but the truths they illustrated are relevant to every culture.

He claimed to be the only way to God

I remember chatting to a French student in a coffee shop. He said that it really didn't matter what you believe, because Jesus was just a good man, like many other religious leaders.

We turned to some verses in John's Gospel, which included Jesus' claim 'I am the way and the truth and the life. No-one comes to the Father except through me.'[5] As he realized the exclusiveness of Jesus' claims, his expression changed. 'Jesus was not a good man,' he exclaimed. 'He was a very arrogant man to say something like that!'

Yet that is the point of Jesus' claims. If they are not true, they are incredibly arrogant. But if they are true, they are universally important. For me to make Jesus' claim about myself would be egotistical and arrogant in the extreme.

He claimed to be God

Just a few sentences after this claim comes an even more staggering statement. Jesus said, 'Anyone who has seen me has seen the Father.'[6] ('Father' is one of the titles used frequently in John's Gospel to talk about God.) The implication was that anyone who had seen Jesus had seen God. On many occasions, Jesus says things that only God could say. He forgives sins and speaks with an authority far beyond that of a normal man. Yet these are not just empty words. On each occasion they are backed up by Jesus doing what only God could do. He calms storms, walks on water and feeds thousands with a packed lunch. The implication is that Jesus is God with a human face.

He claimed to have the answer to death

Later in Jesus' ministry, he visited the tomb of a close friend. The bereaved family stood around, distraught at their sudden loss. Jesus didn't offer the normal words of condolence usually heard in such settings. Instead he stated, 'I am the resurrection and the life.'[7] Imagine if I were to make that kind of claim at a funeral service. It wouldn't go down too well. Yet Jesus not only said it but backed it up, by showing his power over death. He raised the dead man to life.

Unlike many religious leaders, Jesus does not merely offer teaching about death. He claims that he is the hope in the face of death.

He claimed that all the world should follow his teaching

At the end of Jesus' ministry on earth, he gave a job to his followers. He commissioned them to 'go and make disciples of all nations, baptising them . . . and teaching them to obey everything I have commanded you'.[8] Jesus fully expected them to take his teaching to the whole world, and that all should follow it.

Imagine if I were to do the same. I could come up with four pieces of teaching that I think are really good:

- Everyone should support Leicester Tigers Rugby Team.
- People should eat two slices of toast with strawberry jam for breakfast.
- Mushrooms taste of rubber. They are evil and should not be eaten.
- Everyone should wear short-sleeved blue checked shirts on Sundays.

How would you feel if I told everyone reading this book to travel the world and teach all people to obey my teaching? Such a suggestion would be ludicrous. The teaching may be very good (after all, mushrooms are horrible), but I have no right to think that the world should follow my teaching. I would be claiming to have universal authority. Yet that is what Jesus claimed.

He claimed that your attitude to him affects your eternal destiny

In conversation with a very religious man Jesus once said, 'Just as Moses lifted up the snake in the desert, so the Son of Man must be lifted up, that everyone who believes in him may have eternal life.'[9] Jesus is referring to something recorded in the Old Testament part of the Bible. The nation of Israel had rebelled against God and, as a result, had found themselves under his judgment. Poisonous snakes had bitten many people, and a large number of them had died. Realizing the implication of their rebellion, they cried out to God for mercy. So God instructed Moses to make a bronze snake and put it on a pole. Everyone who was bitten and looked at the snake lived. Jesus' claim is that, just as looking at the bronze snake was the only hope for the people bitten by the snakes, believing in him is the only hope for us today. All of humanity stands by default in a position where we justly face the condemnation of God for our rejection of him. Jesus says that our only hope is to believe in him. It is a matter of life and death.

By saying this, Jesus is making a claim that, if true, affects absolutely everyone who has ever lived. C. S. Lewis said, 'Christianity is a statement which, if false, is of no importance, and if true is of infinite importance. The one thing that it cannot be is moderately important.'[10]

One thing we can't say

Jesus' claims are so huge and far-reaching that we cannot dismiss them as having little importance. Yet this is the mistake that Richard Dawkins makes in concluding that Jesus could have been 'honestly mistaken'.[11] Such huge claims could not be made by someone 'honestly mistaken'. They are the words of a madman, a bad man, or God himself. The result is that Christianity is either incredibly important for everyone alive on planet earth, or a foolish delusion based on a lie. We can't dismiss Christianity and yet hold on to Jesus as a good teacher or a moral example. You cannot separate the two. Jesus' claims are so big that, if they are not true, he is neither good nor moral.

In the film *Armageddon*, it is discovered that the whole earth is about to be blown away by a huge asteroid on a collision course with our small green planet. News of the world's imminent destruction travels quickly by TV and radio around the globe. It doesn't matter where people are – the Sahara Desert or downtown Manhattan – everyone is affected. Everyone knows that this news is universally relevant. Ignoring it won't change the situation. No one can say that they are 'not really into asteroids'. (Of course, this being a Hollywood blockbuster, global disaster is avoided at the last moment and the world is saved.)

In the same way as news of a rogue asteroid would have global implications, Jesus' claims have universal importance. They cannot be relevant only for a few, or for a certain era. If they are true, then they affect you and me, and it's vital that we consider them seriously.

However, it is important that we don't simply think of Jesus as being like some big asteroid that is threatening planet earth. Right after Jesus' words about the danger of facing God's judgment, we read: 'For God so loved the world that he gave his one and only Son, that whoever believes in him shall not perish but have eternal life. For God did not send his Son into the world to condemn the world, but to save the world through him.'[12] Jesus did not come to condemn the world. His coming did not put us in danger. He simply alerted us to the danger that we were already in because of our rebellion against God. Jesus came to save the world. He came to offer hope to those who don't deserve it.

Our *greatest* need is not for health, money, stable government, education, or entertainment. If it were, then God could have sent a doctor, an economist, a politician, a professor, or a comedian. Our greatest need is to be rescued from the consequences of our rejection of God. That is why God sent a rescuer.

God is not outdated, out of touch or old-fashioned. The claims of Jesus are so big that they have universal relevance.

They deal with the very heart of the human problem through every generation. Listening to what God has to say will help us make sense of the world we live in today. Unlike the strange traditions of some Christians, Jesus' words are not old-fashioned. They are still relevant and will never go out of date.

3. RAPE, CHILD ABUSE AND AIDS

What kind of God doesn't prevent suffering?

By the time you have finished reading this chapter, 750 women will have become victims of sexual violence, 1,000 children will have been abused (two of them fatally) and forty-five people will have died of AIDS.[1] The statistics are horrific. It is difficult to get our heads around suffering on such a scale.

I was staying at a friend's house recently. A book on the coffee table caught my eye. It told the story of the twentieth century in photos, with several pages devoted to each year. On nearly every page were pictures of war, violence and bloodshed. After a few minutes I had to put it down. There was not a single year free from violence and pain. On average, during the twentieth century, nearly twice as many people died violent deaths around the world *every day* as lost their lives in the 11 September 2001 terrorist attacks.[2] This century shows few signs of being better.

Suffering is not just a statistic. At some point in life, it affects us all. The longer we live, the more of it we experience.

Suffering is not a problem only for Christians. We all have to face up to it.

Some people react to suffering by denying the very possibility of God's existence. If God exists, surely he would have done something about the mess our world is in?

Yet, while I can understand why we might think this way, simply denying the existence of God doesn't get rid of the questions. In fact it leaves us with even more. As we saw earlier, without God what basis do we have for saying that anything is ultimately good or bad? Why should we be so upset at what we see happening around us, and why should we expect anything better? As Richard Dawkins puts it:

> In a universe of blind physical forces and genetic replications some people are going to get lucky and some people are going to get hurt and we won't find any rhyme or reason to it, nor any justice. The universe we observe has precisely the properties we should expect if there is at the bottom no design, no purpose, no evil and no good. Nothing but blind pitiless indifference. DNA neither knows nor cares. DNA just is and we dance to its music.[3]

Are we content to say that there is ultimately no evil and no good? Each day, we see pictures of war, famine and disease on the news and feel that the world shouldn't be this way. We were made for more than this. As we sit with a dying friend, something inside us tells us that it wasn't meant to be like this.

Another way to deal with suffering and evil is not to deny God's existence, but to doubt his goodness. God may exist, but if he does, then the presence of suffering suggests that he cannot be good. The argument goes something like this: If there is a good and powerful God, he would be both willing and able to stop suffering. Yet he hasn't. So a good *and* powerful God can't exist.

However, there is another possibility. God could be both good and powerful, but yet have reasons for allowing suffering that we might not have thought of.

God allows suffering

The opening chapters of the Bible tell us that God created the world. While people may debate the exact details of how that happened, the central truth is clear: God created it, and it was good. Suffering and evil were not part of that world. It was a world as it was meant to be, the kind of world that we long for. No sickness or suffering. No conflict or war.

To live in the good world that God made, he created people. These too were good. In fact, after creating humans God describes his creation as 'very good'.[4] God gave the people he had made real responsibility and freedom. They could live under his gracious rule and enjoy life as it was designed to be lived, or they had the freedom to live their own way and reject him.

Why would God give people that choice? Why make it possible for them to turn away from him? At one level, we are never told. The Bible simply says that this is the way it was. However, our own experiences of life may help us to understand more. For love to be real there must be the freedom not to love. Without choice, there can be no real love.

Imagine it is Valentine's Day. A girl receives a bunch of red roses from her boyfriend. 'Oh, you didn't have to!' she exclaims. 'But I did,' he replies in a matter-of-fact sort of way. 'I didn't have a choice. It's Valentine's Day, and I was just doing what you have to do.' Such a relationship probably won't last very long! For love to be real, it has to be more than a duty.

The Bible says that God loves us. In his love, he created us with the ability freely to return his love. Not to give that choice would be like creating some sort of sophisticated robot. It is because God loves us that he gave us the dignity of that choice.

One of my favourite films is *The Truman Show*. The main character, Truman, is the star of a reality TV show, but he doesn't know it. Ever since he was born, he has lived in a giant film set, which he thinks is a town called Seahaven. Apart from Truman, everyone else in the show is an actor. His wife, his work colleagues and his mates are all actors following the director's script. They have no freedom to do what they want. As the film goes on, you realize that Truman's relationships aren't real. They feel plastic. We long for Truman to escape from this fake world into the real one.

When God created the world, he did not make a giant Seahaven. The people he made were not simply given the script and told to read their lines. God created people with freedom and choice. The tragedy of the history of the world is that people take the freedom they have been given and abuse it. Rather than use it to enjoy God's good world and return his love, we end up abusing it and hurting others.

It is so easy to look at the suffering in our world and blame God. Yet we should not blame God for giving us freedom. It would be like a man blaming his affair on the fact that his wife allowed him to leave the house. God gave us freedom, but we are responsible for the way we have used it.

Who is to blame?

Just after I finished school, I worked for a year at W. H. Smith. One of the worst parts of my job was manning the customer service desk. It was there that, among other things, I had to deal with people who wanted to bring back faulty items. They were often quite angry and usually wanted their money back. I was taught that when I inspected the item, I had to decide whether the problem was due to a manufacturing fault or to misuse by the owner. Who was to blame? If it was the manufacturer, it was a full refund, but if it was the owner it resulted in half an hour's argument and a call to the manager!

When we look at our world, we have to ask the same question: manufacturing fault, or misuse by the owner? We have already seen that the world God made was good. The problem in our world lies with the people who live in it.

A man chatting to his friend said, 'I want to ask God why there is so much suffering and injustice in the world when he could do something about it.' His friend responded, 'I'm worried that God might ask me the same question.' Much of the suffering in our world is caused directly by human beings. It is not God who walks into schools and shoots students. It is not God who kidnaps toddlers and rapes and abuses children. All these things are done by people who have rejected God and lived in their own way. Even famines would not cause the suffering they do, were it not for the greed and selfishness of those in wealthier nations.

There is, however, some suffering for which no one seems to be responsible. Who is responsible for tsunamis, hurricanes and flooding? Who takes the blame for cancer, Down's syndrome, Aids or Alzheimer's disease?

The Bible explains that all these things are evidence that we live in a world that has gone wrong. When humanity rebelled against God, it had catastrophic consequences not only for ourselves but for the world in which we live. Creation carries the scars of sin. The world has been 'subjected to frustration' and 'groaning in the pains of childbirth', as one of the Bible's writers put it.[5]

The metaphor of childbirth reminds us that suffering need not be an end in itself. The hope for a mother in labour is that the pain will lead to the joy of a new life. In the same way, the Bible gives us hope that, although we suffer now, this need not be the end of the story. The world we live in is not what it once was; but neither is it what it will one day be.

God will end suffering

Surely, if God is powerful and loving, he could get rid of the evil and suffering we experience? But it is important to consider where the evil and suffering come from. We can be quick to blame the problems of the world on politicians, dictators, terrorists, insurgents and criminals.

Jesus says that the real problem of the world is not confined to prisons or parliaments. It is much more widespread than that. 'From within, out of men's hearts, come evil thoughts, sexual immorality, theft, murder, adultery, greed, malice, deceit, lewdness, envy, slander, arrogance and folly.'[6] The heart of the problem is our hearts. For a loving God to get rid of evil is not as simple as we might think.

The heart of the problem is our hearts.

I often ask people, 'If you were God and you wanted to end the suffering and pain of the world, who would you get rid of first?' Normally terrorists, rapists, child abusers and murderers come top of the list. But what if all these criminals were taken out of the world? Would it then be a perfect place? Who else should we throw out? People normally suggest thieves, hooligans, used-car salesmen and traffc wardens. But would the world be perfect then? Who else should we get rid of?

Slowly, the realization dawns: somewhere down the line, we fit in too. We can hurt others through the things we do and say. Sometimes it is our failure to do what we should do that causes the problem. We know from painful experience that it is not only terrorists and dictators who can cause us pain. It can be those we love, and we are aware that we are all too capable of doing the same. So often, in our selfishness, we end up hurting those closest to us. Ultimately we see that we are part of the problem. But of course, we don't want God to get rid of *us*. We want God to sort the world out, but we don't want him to sort *us* out.

Once some people came to Jesus and asked his opinion on a tragedy that had just taken place. There had been a massacre in the nearby region of Galilee. Perhaps at the back of the questioners' minds was the thought that these Galileans had done something particularly evil, to deserve such a death. People can ask the same question today about those who die in national tragedies: is the death of such people a judgment for some particular sin they have committed?

Jesus' answer shows this is a wrong way of thinking: 'Do you think that these Galileans were worse sinners than all the other Galileans because they suffered this way? I tell you, no!'[7] From this we can see that we shouldn't think of suffering as a punishment for specific sins that we have committed.

However, what Jesus goes on to say is quite shocking: 'But unless you repent, you too will all perish.'[8] While suffering is not to be viewed as a specific punishment for sin, we shouldn't think we are innocent, either. Jesus is saying that we are *all* guilty people who deserve punishment. This goes against what we so often think – that we are basically good people who deserve God's blessings. Jesus teaches that all of humanity stands in a perilous situation. We deserve the judgment of God and need to turn from living our own way and back to him.

Jesus teaches that all of humanity stands in a perilous situation.

So why doesn't God exercise that judgment now? Later on in the Bible, we find the answer: 'He [God] is patient with you, not wanting anyone to perish, but everyone to come to repentance.'[9] While God in his justice would be perfectly fair in punishing us for our sin, in his love he is patient with us, wanting us to turn back to him and find the forgiveness he offers. Every day that this world continues is a sign of God's patience with those who live in it. God could put an end to it now, but where would that leave us?

It is because God is patient that he hasn't yet done away with evil and suffering. He is giving people an opportunity to turn back to him. Before he changes the world, he needs to change us.

God has experienced suffering

All this may help us to understand why God allows suffering in the world and why he hasn't yet brought it to an end. But does it help when we come to suffer ourselves? How do we cope when we ourselves are going through pain? C. S. Lewis wrote a book about suffering, *The Problem of Pain*. After it was published, he lost his own wife to cancer. He later wrote another book entitled *A Grief Observed*. While both books deal with the same subject, pain and suffering, they do so in very different ways. For someone going through it, suffering is not an intellectual problem but an emotional one.

When we ourselves suffer, we feel that we want more than answers. We want someone who understands, and who can stand with us. But what does God know about suffering? Many Eastern world views see suffering as an illusion, while Western religions often picture God as distant and removed. Only Christianity tells us of a God who has experienced our suffering. One writer put it this way:

I could never myself believe in God if it were not for the cross
. . . In the real world of pain, how could one worship a God
who was immune to it? I have entered many Buddhist temples
. . . and stood respectfully before the statue of the Buddha,
his legs crossed, arms folded, eyes closed, the ghost of a smile
playing around his mouth . . . detached from the agonies of
the world. But each time after a while I have had to turn away.
And in my imagination I have turned instead to that lonely,
twisted, tortured figure on the cross, nails through hands and
feet, back lacerated, limbs wrenched, brow bleeding from
thorn-pricks, mouth dry and intolerably thirsty, plunged in
God-forsaken darkness. That is the God for me! He laid aside
his immunity to pain. He entered our world of flesh and
blood, tears and death. He suffered for us.[10]

God is able to identify with us in our suffering because he
himself, as a human, has experienced what this world is like.
His birth was seen by many as illegitimate. He was brought
up as a refugee. He lived and worked in a land under cruel
foreign occupation. His own family misunderstood him, his
friends deserted him and one of his followers betrayed him.
He experienced the most terrible injustice. He went through
horrific torture and died an agonizing death.

When we suffer, God knows what it is like. He is not like
well-meaning friends, who might claim to empathize when
in reality they can't. God has suffered in the most horrific way.
He knows pain from the inside and can empathize with us
in ours.

More than empathy

Jesus' suffering means that he can identify with ours. But
identification alone does not actually change our situation. It
is as if I meet somebody who has a headache. Without a

headache myself, I cannot identify with them in theirs. Of course, I could bang my head against a brick wall and get one too. However, I haven't done anything about the other person's situation. We simply have two headaches: one each. When it comes to suffering, we want more than empathy; we want to know that something can be done about it.

Jesus' death was more than simply identification with us in our suffering. As Jesus died, he was dealing with the root cause of suffering, which is our sin. He took upon himself the evil and wrong of the world and bore the punishment that we deserve. Because of the cross, we can be forgiven by God and brought into relationship with him.

In the face of suffering and evil, the cross of Jesus is the greatest hope available. Here is a God who not only understands and feels our pain, but also willingly takes our sin, guilt and shame, so that we can be forgiven.

Author and speaker James Sire lost his father to cancer. After watching him die in horrible agony, he was left wondering how God could have allowed his dad to go through such a terrible experience. How could he, James, come to terms with what had happened – what did his Christian faith give him in that time of trial? He concludes:

> I am drawn to Jesus. He has gone through such pain as
> no other human being has ever experienced. He took on
> himself all the sins of the world, my father's sins, my sins,
> and he bore for both of us the experience of separation
> from God. He who called God *Abba*, Daddy, found himself
> abandoned. 'God made him who had no sin to be sin for
> us, so that in him we might become the righteousness of
> God' . . . I cannot fathom such love. I cannot say to a God
> who has done this that he has treated me or my father
> wrongly.[11]

This does not mean that we have all the answers to our questions. Yet what we do know helps us to trust God with what we don't. The cross does not tell us why an all-powerful God would allow specific suffering in our lives. Yet it does show us what the answer is not: it cannot be that he doesn't love us. If God was willing to go to such lengths to rescue me so that I could be forgiven, can I say that he doesn't love me? One Bible writer put it this way: 'He who did not spare his own Son, but gave him up for us all – how will he not also, along with him, graciously give us all things?'[12]

Amazing hope

Suffering is not the end of the story. The Bible also looks to the future. The amazing promise of the Bible is that because of Jesus' death and resurrection, suffering will one day be history. The penultimate chapter of the Bible describes the hope that awaits those who have trusted in Jesus' death for their forgiveness:

> Then I saw a new heaven and a new earth, for the first heaven and the first earth had passed away . . . I heard a loud voice from the throne saying, 'Now the dwelling of God is with men, and he will live with them. They will be his people, and God himself will be with them and be their God. He will wipe away every tear from their eyes. There will be no more death or mourning or crying or pain, for the old order of things has passed away.'
>
> He who was seated on the throne said, 'I am making everything new!'[13]

Reading a description like this is like sniffng the aroma of a delicious meal when we are ravenously hungry, or glimpsing a photo of a glorious summer's day on a wet January morning. We can only imagine what it will be like.

The Bible says that 'our present sufferings are not worth comparing with the glory that will be revealed in us'.[14] Those words were written by someone who had experienced a life of suffering and discomfort. The suffering of this world is real and painful, but it doesn't even bear comparison with what God will one day bring about.

God is not uncaring or callous. He is not to blame for the suffering we experience in this world. One day he will end it all. In the meantime, he knows what suffering is like and can be with us in ours.

4. CARBON FOOTPRINTS, GLOBAL WARMING AND CLIMATE CHANGE

What kind of God doesn't care about his creation?

A recent newspaper report ahead of a global conference on climate change revealed yet more South Pacific islands being threatened by rising sea levels. For instance, Tuvalu, with its highest point only 5 metres above current sea level, could be completely submerged by the end of the century if current rising sea levels continue as predicted.[1] The actions of industrialized nations thousands of miles away could soon mean that the islanders will have no islands left.

However, it is not just islands in the South Pacific that would be affected. A 7-metre rise in sea levels would make cities like London uninhabitable. A recent poll of 45,000 people revealed that, globally, climate change is seen as the biggest threat to our world.[2] In a recent BBC news report on the subject, the Governor of the Bank of England warned that the challenges currently posed by climate change 'pale in significance compared with what might come'.[3]

The reasons for such a gloomy outlook are clear. Dramatically increasing carbon emissions are making a massive impact on the environment. Energy consumption is rocketing as developing countries catch up with the rest of the world. It is predicted that by the end of the century there will be a 350% increase in carbon emissions, while every day the equivalent of 71,000 football fields of natural forest are being destroyed.

A few years ago, climate change seemed to be the concern of only a vocal minority. The majority of the population continued to live without making any real change in their lifestyle or habits. Today the opposite is the case. The environment is regularly in the news and all the main political parties are talking about it, and not without reason. A few years ago the threat to our environment seemed distant and imperceptible. Now we can see the effects of climate change at first hand.

In a culture where environmental concern is important, belief in God can often seem like an excuse for doing nothing. The USA, for instance, viewed by many as a predominantly 'Christian' nation, has often been reluctant to face up to the issue of climate change. As a country, it represents just 4.5% of the world's population, but is responsible for 14% of the world's total carbon emissions.[4] Ironically, one government official suggested that the best way to deal with global warming was to install more air conditioning!

Christians too seem to have drawn a divide between the physical and the spiritual. It appears that God is more interested in a person's inner spirituality than in practical matters such as the environment. But what use are reading the Bible, praying and singing, when the world around us is being destroyed? Surely we should be planting trees, recycling rubbish and conserving energy?

Another issue is the Bible's teaching about the end of the world. If our world will ultimately be destroyed, why bother to look after the environment? If I knew my block of flats was going to be demolished tomorrow, I wouldn't waste money repainting my living room today. As a previous US Secretary of the Interior once said: 'We don't have to protect the environment; the second coming is at hand.'[5]

In view of these examples, it is easy to see why people may blame belief in God for many of the environmental problems we are facing. Surely we should forget about the Bible's God when it comes to the environment, as it seems that other world views are much better equipped to protect it?

For instance, pantheism is the view that God is within nature, so this would seem to give us more incentive to care for it. If God not only made the tree but is the tree itself, this would make you think twice before chopping it down! Scientific naturalists who emphasize the wonder of the material world may also appear to have more reason to look after the environment. After all, if what we see around us is all we have got, then we had better look after it.

What does the Bible say God thinks about his creation?

God cares about the environment

As we read through the Bible, three major events in the storyline reveal God's concern for the physical world.

God created a physical world

The Bible teaches that God is responsible for the physical world in which we live. All life originates from him. In the account of God's creating work, we are repeatedly told that what God had made 'was good'.[6] His seal of approval was given to the physical world. Rainforests and rivers, mountains and oceans were all his idea.

The world we live in shows staggering creativity and diversity, reflecting something of the glory of its Creator.

Worshipping God is far more than simply going to a building and singing songs. It involves every area of life. It means appreciating the world that God has made and delighting in it. Sitting on a beach and enjoying a glorious sunset, or standing in awe at the view from a mountain summit can be acts of worship. I can worship God as I ski down a mountain in Switzerland or windsurf in Poole Harbour. God is interested in the whole of his creation and wants us to be so, too.

However, the goodness of the world has been marred and spoilt. Human rebellion against its Creator had massive implications for the natural world. The Bible looks forward to the day when the 'creation itself will be liberated from its bondage to decay and brought into the glorious freedom of the children of God'.[7] In the meanwhile, even though the world is broken, God still shows his care for the creation by giving instructions on how to look after it. The Old Testament warns against cruelty to livestock and advocates care for physical things such as trees and plants.

God becomes physical

When we move into the New Testament, we discover the stunning fact that the God who created the physical world stepped into it. Not only as a spirit, but as a real physical person. The Bible says that in Jesus God 'became flesh'.[8] Jesus' physical nature is emphasized when John, one of his followers, talks about him as the one 'we have seen with our eyes . . . we have looked at and our hands have touched'.[9]

The fact that God became a physical person has huge implications for the way we should view our world. Some early sects of Christianity taught that the material world is evil, while the spiritual world is good. Jesus shows that this view is wrong, because the two are not to be separated. By taking on a physical human nature God shows approval for this physical world. The material world is not an evil to be avoided, but a gift to be enjoyed and looked after.

A real and physical hope

This physical creation is not merely temporary, either. The Bible's hope for the future is also very real and physical. We can know this because of the resurrection of Jesus.

The Gospel writers make it clear that, when Jesus rose from the dead, it wasn't just in some spiritual or metaphorical way. His resurrection body was physical – he could eat, touch, see and speak. The Bible goes on to teach that Jesus' resurrection is the prototype of what Christians will receive: that is, real physical bodies.

This is very different from many people's preconceptions of a fluffy, floating, cloudlike existence. Physical bodies can't live on clouds; they would fall through them! Physical bodies need a physical world, and that is what the Bible looks forward to. The book of Revelation talks about not only a new heaven, but a new earth.

So the physical creation is not evil, nor is it simply a temporary realm on the way to a merely spiritual home. A physical and material world was – and always will be – God's idea. It was good, and one day it will be made new.

We should care about the environment

So how does this affect the way people should view the physical world? How does it change our attitude to the environment?

The right motivation?

Caring for the environment is not something that is uniquely Christian. One TV documentary discussed how to encourage people to be more environmentally aware. It seems there are several different ways to motivate people:

- The financial factor: making it more expensive to pollute by taxing fuel and flying
- The family factor: telling people how terrible the world will be for their grandchildren if they don't change their habits
- The fear factor: telling people how terrible the world will be for *them* if they don't change their habits
- The fashion factor: making environmentalism fashionable and so encouraging people to look good in front of others by cycling to work and recycling their rubbish.

The problem with all of these factors is that they play on my selfishness to make me change: the love I have for *my* money, *my* family, *my* future, or *my* image. They all affect *me*. That is why the media often emphasize the immediate effects of global warming, because what affects me now will be more persuasive than what affects my great-grandchildren in a hundred years' time.

If there is no God, there is no ultimate motivation for caring about the environment. It is just an accident. We may want to look after it, but we have no ultimate moral basis for doing so and no real reason to be upset when others don't do so either. Pantheism doesn't really help. If the world is to be identified with God, any seeming problem with the natural world must therefore be an illusion. The answer then becomes transcending the illusion, rather than trying to fix the planet by practical means.

In contrast to this, the Bible's teaching about God gives us real and authentic motivation to care for the environment. It does so by showing us what our relationships should be with both the creation and its Creator.

Leasehold not freehold

Having always rented my flat, I didn't know much about the property market. However, when I started to look into buying my own place, I soon discovered a number of interesting things, not least that it is possible to buy a house and yet still not really own it. Buying a house on a leasehold agreement means that the house is mine to enjoy and look after, potentially for the rest of my life. However, someone else still holds the ultimate right over it.[10]

The Bible teaches that our relationship with this world is not too dissimilar. In one place we read, 'The earth is the LORD's, and everything in it,'[11] while in another it says, 'the earth he [God] has given to man'.[12]

Who does the world belong to? On one level it belongs to us, but ultimately it is God's. We are to live as stewards in God's world, as we look after it. God gave humanity a position of responsibility and dominion, but not domination.

If you hired a car for the day, you might be tempted to burn some rubber and see how fast it could go. You might not worry too much about how you treated it. After all, it is not yours and you don't personally know the owner. However, if you borrowed a car from a good friend, I would expect that your attitude might be different. Knowing the person who owned it would mean that you would treat it with respect.

In the same way, knowing the God who created the world means treating what he has given us with care and respect. Our attitude towards this physical world reveals something of our attitude to God. We have no excuse for abusing or spoiling it. Caring about the environment and working to preserve it is part of what it means to live under God's authority. Whether or not my care for the environment were to have any impact upon me personally, I should still do it. The Bible doesn't motivate us to action through an appeal to our selfishness, but rather to our God-given responsibility.

What we do now lasts for eternity

However, it may still seem like fighting a losing battle. If the world is going to be made new in the end why worry too much about this old one? It might seem like trying to fix a car that is going to be scrapped anyway. But if we use that logic in other areas of life, we can see how silly it is.

If you bought a bunch of flowers for someone you love, you wouldn't, I hope, see it as a futile exercise. Just because the flowers will eventually die doesn't mean that it is not a good thing to do. Although the enjoyment is only temporary, the action is real, and even when the flowers have died, the goodness of it remains.

In the same way, our actions in this world have eternal consequences. Speaking about people who have died, the Bible says that 'their deeds will follow them'.[13] We shouldn't think only about seemingly 'spiritual' actions such as praying and Bible reading. For the Christian, nothing is wasted. Planting a tree, insulating a house, recycling rubbish and cycling to work are not pointless exercises.

Starting today

Knowing that the Bible promises a physical new creation should also be an encouragement to look after this one well. Caring for the environment and looking after the world is not something we do for only a temporary period of time. It will continue into the new creation, too. Far from removing the motivation, this should encourage us to be involved in it right now.

God is not to blame for the environmental problems we face today. He not only created the world but cares about it. The environment matters to God, and it should matter to us too. He is grieved when it is ruined by selfishness and greed. God is concerned for the whole of life, not just for what we do on Sundays. Living his way means rediscovering the purpose for which we were made. That will mean having the privilege of looking after God's creation, both now and for eternity.

5. CRUSADES, INQUISITIONS AND CAR BOMBS

What kind of God allows violence in his name?

'More people have been killed in the name of Jesus Christ than [in the name of] anyone else in history' claims the American author Gore Vidal. So it is not surprising that you might be tempted to think that a world without religion would be a better place to live in. Christopher Hitchens goes as far as to say 'Religion poisons everything. As well as a menace to civilization, it has become a threat to human survival.'[1] Oscar Wilde commented, 'When I think of all the harm the Bible has done, I despair of ever writing anything equal to it.'

> Imagine, with John Lennon, a world with no religion. Imagine no suicide bombers, no 9/11, no 7/7, no crusades, no witch-hunts, no Gunpowder Plot, no Indian partition, no Israeli/Palestinian wars, no Serb/Croat/Muslim massacres, no persecution of Jews as 'Christ-killers', no shiny bouffant-haired televangelists fleecing gullible people of their money ('God wants you to give till it hurts'). Imagine no Taliban to blow

up ancient statues, no public beheadings of blasphemers, no flogging of female skin for the crime of showing an inch of it.[2]

At least, that is what Richard Dawkins would like us to imagine at the beginning of his best-selling book *The God Delusion*.

Since the 9/11 terrorist attacks, the question of religious violence has never been far from the headlines. Despite what some politicians say, it hard to imagine that recent terrorist attacks in Paris, Beirut and Mali (to name just a few) have nothing whatsoever to do with religion. Yet despite being such a current problem, it is certainly not a new issue. Over 300 years ago, the French philosopher Blaise Pascal declared that 'Men never do evil so completely and cheerfully as when they do it from religious conviction.'[3]

One of the problems of looking at a subject like this is that it is often difficult to remain objective. The whole subject of war is so emotive that it is easy to exaggerate, making claims that are not true. For instance, in Dan Brown's *The Da Vinci Code*, the claim is made that six million women were killed during the Inquisition. The actual number was many fewer, not all the victims were women and not all the killings were carried out by the church. That is not to say that such actions are excusable, but, on another level, neither is exaggeration of the truth.

In 2006 Richard Dawkins presented a series of programmes on Channel 4 entitled *The Root of all Evil*. In his book published afterwards, he actually explains that he doesn't quite believe that religion is in fact the root of *all* evil. However, we get the impression that he wasn't *too* upset about the title.

So is religion the root cause of most of the conflict in our world? Does belief in God inevitably lead to violence and conflict?

The root of *all* evil?

Just a brief glance over the last century shows that two regimes that perpetrated incredible amounts of violence were not inspired by religion. Hitler's National Socialism and Communism were inspired by the atheistic philosophies of Nietzsche and Marx respectively. I frequently travel to Romania and have heard at first hand heart-breaking and horrific stories of the suffering experienced by many of the Christians there during the Communist era. To say that atheism had nothing to do with this is incredibly naïve – it was precisely because of the atheistic ideology that Christians were often physically and mentally persecuted, in an attempt to force them to deny their belief in God. Getting rid of religion certainly won't remove all conflict, however persuasively atheists like Dawkins and Hitchens may argue.

Religion is not the only motivation for war. When I was at secondary school my maths teacher once mocked me for being a Christian. 'Half the world's wars are caused by religion,' he claimed, 'so I am having nothing to do with it!' Perhaps unwisely, I responded by asking, 'If money also causes war, are you going to have nothing to do with that, either?'

What is religion?

It is also important to consider how we define religion. It may be popular to say that all religions are really the same. The truth is that, even on the most basic levels, they disagree. Buddhists do not believe in God at all, while Hindus believe in many gods and Christians believe in one God. To say that 'religion' in general causes violence is to fail to see that there are massive differences between religions. Religion can cause violence, but so too can any world view or philosophy. So, while we may not consider ourselves religious, we all have values and beliefs that we live our lives by. These may not be offcially formulated, or even have a name, but they will profoundly affect the way we live. Getting rid of organized religion will not eliminate absolute beliefs.

Oxford professor and writer Alister McGrath explains, 'when a society rejects the idea of God, it tends to transcendentalize alternatives [to make something else absolute and unquestionable, in the place of God] – such as the ideals of liberty and equality. These now become quasi-divine authorities, which none are permitted to challenge.'[4] He goes on to quote the example of Madame Roland, who was executed during the French Revolution – a time when traditional ideas about God had been rejected in favour of human ideals and values. As she stepped up to the guillotine she bowed mockingly to the statue of Liberty and uttered the now famous words 'O liberty, liberty, what crimes are committed in your name!' Any system of values and beliefs is open to abuse, whether it is grounded in belief in God or not. Simply doing away with traditional religions will not prevent this.

Any system of values and beliefs is open to abuse

A question of consistency

Asking whether religion in general causes violence is the wrong question, because it is clear that religion does, but so also do many other philosophies and ideologies. Rather, we need to ask: when acts of violence have been committed, were the people responsible acting consistently with what they believed? In other words, was violence the *natural outworking* of their beliefs?

This would be a good question to ask about every case of violence, whether perpetrated by people claiming to be Christian, Muslim, atheist, or anything else. However, here I want to focus more specifically on the charges levelled against Christianity. What are we to make of the record of Christians, and what does this tell us about their God?

Bad representatives

Imagine that a group of my friends decide to form a Queen tribute band. They are enthusiastic and passionate about Queen's music, but there is just one problem: they can't sing or play! However, ignoring the advice of others, they proceed to hire the local pub for their first performance. Thankfully, most people are wise enough to avoid the venue on the night in question – but not everyone. There just happens to be a group of Mongolian students on a three-week exchange visit at the university. Having nothing to do, and no knowledge either of the band Queen or of my friends' musical abilities, they head down to the Pig and Whistle to find out more. Their experience is not a pleasant one. After about five minutes, they make a quick exit and go as far away from the pub as possible. His ears still ringing with one of the worst ever renditions of 'Bohemian Rhapsody', one of the students is heard to say, 'Queen are the worst band in the world. I never ever want to hear anything by them again.'

It's easy to realize why the students might feel this way. Yet this does not mean that they have come to the right conclusion. Having heard a very bad representation of a piece by a great band, they have been put off ever hearing any more. Unfortunately the same is true of many people's impressions

of Christianity. Having been put off by many bad representatives of Jesus, they never take time to look at the real thing.

Sadly, there are many occasions in history where people
have claimed the name of Christ but have acted in ways that
are utterly inconsistent with his example. This has happened
for several reasons.

Misunderstanding Jesus

Sometimes this has been due to people misunderstanding the
true nature of Christianity. This was certainly true of the
Crusades, which were motivated by a political view of Christianity. Those responsible believed that expanding Christ's
kingdom meant reclaiming Palestine from the Muslims. In
complete contrast, Jesus taught that faith in him was not tied
to politics and places. The important thing is not where we
are geographically, but who we are spiritually.

This is revealed in a conversation that Jesus once had with
a woman from a different religion. She wanted to know where
people should worship. Was it with the Jews in Jerusalem, or
nearby on another mountain, where her family worshipped?
Jesus explained that it was 'neither on this mountain, nor in
Jerusalem . . . a time is coming and has now come when the
true worshippers will worship the Father in spirit and truth'.[5]

Jesus' words show that true worship does not require us to
be in a certain geographical place, or part of a 'Christian
nation'. There is no such thing as a Christian nation – just
Christian people who live in many nations. The basis of our
faith is not a place but a person: Jesus.

It wasn't only Christians in the Middle Ages who misunderstood Jesus. The Bible records that even his first followers
sometimes did the same. When they discovered that Jesus was
the Messiah (the long-awaited King that God had promised to
send), they too jumped to the wrong conclusion. Immediately

they presumed that he was to be a political leader, come to set them free from Roman rule and bring peace and prosperity. That is why they were so shocked when Jesus announced that, rather than killing his enemies, he was going to die for them.[6] He wasn't coming to set up a political kingdom, and neither should his followers.

Misinterpreting the Bible

People often point to the fact that the Bible seems to be an inherently violent book, and sometimes this has been used as an excuse for violence. The Old Testament certainly contains accounts of wars, and the New Testament uses the language of battles. However, it is important to read the Bible in the way it was written and to interpret it properly. The Bible is not a flat list of instructions and examples to follow, but rather a story.

The fact that we read in the Old Testament of wars carried out by the nation of Israel is no warrant for a church or nation today to do the same. The wars in the Old Testament were part of God's specific judgment on the evil and wickedness of the surrounding nations. It was not arbitrary, but followed extended periods of God's patience, where people were given the opportunity to turn back to him. The serious treatment was needed in much the same way as chemotherapy would be used on cancer. If evil is not removed, it spreads. We shouldn't think, though, that God simply hated the other nations and gave special exemption to his own people. When the Israelites turned away from God, they too faced judgment at the hands of their enemies. When the other nations turned back to God, they were spared the judgment they would have faced.

When we move forward into the New Testament part of the Bible, we don't find a different God. He is still passionately opposed to evil, but the Old Testament wars pointed forward to a greater judgment that is yet to come. Alongside this we read of God's patience and a way by which we can come back to God. The Bible never gives Christians the right to think that they have a role to exercise judgment in the same way as the Old Testament nation of Israel did.

The New Testament may use the language of war, but it is not to be taken in a literal sense. It clearly says that our battle is not a physical one, against people, but a spiritual one, against evil.[7]

Ulterior motives

Sometimes the actions of professing Christians have been motivated more by secular ambition than by genuine belief. I have travelled many times to Northern Ireland, which was for many years the scene of apparently religious conflict. Yet many people don't realize what motivated those who perpetrated so much of the violence. For many, it had very little to do with real Christianity, but much more with loyalty, revenge and status.

A friend of mine grew up in Belfast and from an early age got involved in a paramilitary group. His activities led to his arrest and several years in the notorious Maze Prison. It wasn't until after his release that he became a real Christian. Looking back, he says, 'I did what I thought at the time was right, but I was wrong. So did the other groups. But two wrongs don't make a right.' He is now the minister of a large church there, and members of his congregation come from both sides of the 'divide'.

Good representatives

Let's go back again to our Mongolian students. Just as there are bad tribute bands, like the one they have just heard, I know there are also some good ones, which look and sound more like the original. If I wanted to repair the damage inflicted by my friends' band, I could take the students to hear a good tribute group. That would give them a much better idea of what Queen were actually like. In the same way, we can also turn to much better representatives of God. By 'better', I don't mean only that their actions are positive and peaceful, but also more consistent with what they believe.

Some Christians, such as William Wilberforce and Martin Luther King, are well known for their positive impact on society. Others may be less well known, but their legacy is still enjoyed today. Health care, free education and the abolition of child labour are all the work of previous generations of Christians. For them, consistent Christianity meant opposing the social evils they found and working tirelessly for positive change.[8]

Yet both Richard Dawkins and Christopher Hitchens seem to be completely blind to the positive influence that Christianity has had on the course of history. In their respective books, such positive influences are swept under the carpet without any consideration. They have drawn their conclusions while ignoring much of the evidence.

Today, many Christians are still working in different parts of the world, trying to bring food to the starving, justice to the oppressed and care to the sick. The church that I am a part of has a special day every year, alongside ongoing projects, when we raise a significant amount of money for a situation in the majority world. Recently we set up an orphanage in Malawi, which we now help to maintain. Consistent Christianity means caring for the poor and needy and working for justice. It is not an accident that these Christians are doing what they are doing, but rather an outworking of their convictions and beliefs.

The real thing

Let's return to our Mongolian friends one final time. While tribute bands can be both good and bad, there is one thing that is even better – the original. If the students really want to know what Queen are like, they need to buy a CD or download an MP3 of the original band. In the same way, if we want to know what real Christianity is like, the best thing to do is look at the One who started it all.

When we take a look at Jesus, we find someone whose teaching is radically opposed to violence and retribution. So when Jesus was rejected by another religious group, his followers suggested bringing about divine vengeance. 'Do you want us to call fire down from heaven to destroy them?'[9] they asked. Jesus' response was not what they expected. Rather than applauding their religious zeal, he rebuked them for not understanding what he was about.

In Jesus' famous Sermon on the Mount he teaches people how they should react to those who oppose them. He says, 'Blessed are the peacemakers . . . Love your enemies'.[10] Anyone who claims to be a Christian and yet stirs up hatred and violence has obviously lost sight of Jesus' radical teaching in this area.

Practise what you preach

Jesus' teaching clearly shows that Christians are to respond to their enemies with love rather than retribution. But was it just talk? Was he consistent with his own teaching? Both religious and political leaders can be well known for saying one thing but doing another. We are sick of nice-sounding talk coming from people whose lives communicate a very different message.

In contrast, when we look at Jesus' life we see someone who is utterly consistent with his own teaching, even to the point of death. Here was a man who practised what he preached even when it hurt. As he was arrested, he rebuked one of his followers who had leapt to his defence wielding a sword. Later, when he was being executed by cruel Roman guards after being tried by an illegal court, he cried out, 'Father, forgive them, for they do not know what they are doing.'[11] Both his teaching and his actions show utter consistency.

Both his teaching and his actions show utter consistency.

As we look at Jesus, and particularly his death on the cross, we see the measuring stick by which we should judge Christianity. To what degree have Christians been consistent with the One they seek to follow? Sadly, at times in their history they have been terribly inconsistent, turning the cross upside down and brandishing it as a sword. However, at other times they have reflected Jesus' example much more clearly.

What we see is that, for Christians, the answer to religious violence is to be *more* consistent, not less. Jesus taught, through both words and example, what it meant really to love even your enemies. Christians need to be more consistent in following him. The degree to which Christians have a positive impact on the world will be directly related to the degree to which they follow Jesus.

Recently I was watching a debate in the House of Commons, where an MP expressed concern at the rise of religious extremism. The point was made that extreme belief in any religion would be a dangerous thing. The suggested answer was that people should hold their beliefs more lightly. Of course, if a belief is inherently violent, then being more moderate is a good thing, and abandoning it altogether would be even better. Yet, as we have seen, Christianity is a belief centred on a person of radical love and forgiveness. So the need is not to be less extreme in following him, but more so.

This has been the case throughout history. So when William Wilberforce campaigned to abolish slavery, he did not ask people to loosen their Christian values, but strengthen them. Likewise Martin Luther King did not ask Christians to take their faith less seriously, but more so, in his fight to end systematic racism in America. The need is for people to be more consistent with Jesus. He showed by his example that God does not condone religious violence, and tells us that we are not merely to tolerate our enemies, but to love them.

What *is* the root of all evil?

So, if the world's problems cannot be blamed on belief in God or a religious system, what is the cause? Jesus identified the source of evil not externally in a religious system, but internally in our hearts.[12]

In describing humans as sinful, the Bible is not suggesting we are all murderers or rapists. Sin is deeper than actions. It is more like a disease that has many different symptoms. At its most fundamental level, sin is an attitude that says, 'I am number one and I deserve to get my way at all costs.' We reject God and set ourselves up in his place.

This was well illustrated when I was in Burger King having dinner a while ago. As I was tucking into my bacon double cheeseburger meal, I read these words on the promotional leaflet on the tray in front of me: 'Have it your way! You have the right to have exactly what you want, exactly when you want it. Because of the menu of life, you are today's special, and tomorrow's and . . . [Well, you get the drift.] That's right, we may be the King, but you, my friend, are the almighty ruler.'

This might sound quite appealing. After all, we like the idea of having it our way. But actually Burger King have described the very problem with our world. We all want it our way and believe it is our right. But what happens when, wanting it our way, we come into conflict with someone who wants it their way? We fight it out. Most of us don't use bombs and guns. Our weapons are words that hurt and looks that kill. We have experienced conflict in our relationships and families, and we know how painful it is. We hate it, yet at the same time we know that sometimes we cause it.

However, when two world leaders disagree and are both convinced that their way is right, it is much more serious. They too fight it out. But this time they have armies at their disposal. If someone doesn't have a big enough army, it no longer seems to matter. They can find other ways of trying to get their way – such as car bombs and aeroplanes.

So why doesn't God get rid of all conflict and war now? Well he could do so, but where should he stop? Why stop with global conflict? What about the conflicts in our own families and friendships? What about the violence in our own hearts? Instead of getting rid of us, God is being patient, allowing us the time to change, to step down from running our lives our own way and come to experience the new life that is found in living his way.

Hope for a broken world

The wonderful hope of Christianity is that God has stepped down into our broken and divided world to do something about it. Jesus experienced violence and pain himself, often at the hands of deeply religious people. Not only did he show us how we should respond to such violence, he did even more. As he died, he took the punishment of God for all the violence and injustice of this world. He made it possible for people like us to be forgiven and brought into a relationship with God.

Wonderfully, the Bible also looks forward to a day in the future when God will make the world new. War and conflict will be history. As one Old Testament prophet put it, 'They will beat their swords into ploughshares and their spears into pruning hooks. Nation will not take up sword against nation, nor will they train for war any more.'[13] The language might sound archaic, but the reality it describes is amazing. The instruments used to kill in war will be used to farm in peace. The weapons of destruction become the tools of production. People will no longer hurt one another but help one another. Here is a wonderful place, where death, pain and tears are history: a brilliant picture of an amazing place.

Throughout history, God has often been badly represented by people who claim to follow him. But God is not to blame for violence and war. Jesus shows us perfectly the attitude we should adopt towards others. The answer to the world's violence is not to get rid of God, but to turn back to him.

6. HYPOCRITICAL, DIVIDED AND JUDGMENTAL

What kind of God lets the church represent him?

'Would you like to come with me to church this Sunday?' I asked a friend. The look on the friend's face was memorable. I think I would have got a better reaction if I had asked him to spend a quiet morning at the mortuary, or an afternoon at the lawn-mower museum. To many, church just doesn't seem very attractive. Given their experience of it, it's not always surprising.

For a start, it seems hypocritical. News reports appear that a priest is found guilty of sexually abusing young boys; a married minister is discovered to have been having a long-term affair; a church treasurer swindles his congregation out of thousands of pounds. It is not that these problems are exclusive to the church, yet for an organization that is seen to be promoting moral values, such behaviour appears to be hypocritical in the extreme.

The church can also seem incredibly divided: there are apparently over 33,000 denominations around the world. That means that, even if I lived my life ten times over, there would still be more denominations than I could ever visit, even if I went to a new one every week.

I was in a newsagents in Cornwall when I noticed the headline on the front of the local newspaper: 'Church splits over organ'. A local church had recently replaced its rotting organ with an electric piano. Not only had the congregation divided over the issue, but one side was threatening to take the other to court.

Just as sad are the judgmental attitudes experienced by some people in their dealings with churches. I remember being given a lift to church one summer evening by the parents of a friend. They asked me if I wanted to go and get ready, but I told them I already was. 'No, you're not,' they replied. 'You're not going to church dressed in *shorts!*' Ironically, it seemed that as long as you were dressed in a suit, driving at over 100mph to get there was fine.

If we get our impression of the church only from the media, then it will probably be a very negative one. The church seems to make the headlines only when some scandal breaks and reveals hypocrisy in its leaders. Church splits and divisions are all too common, and church leaders condemning certain lifestyles and practices give the impression that the church is there only to judge.

It may be that your view of the church has been influenced by your own painful experience of it. As far as you're concerned, your experience was suffciently awful for you never to want to consider it again.

Whatever has influenced our view of the church, we are left with a big problem. Our issue is ultimately not only with the church, but with God himself. We cannot separate the two. The Bible teaches us that, through the church, something of God's character is made known.[1] But considering some of the experiences of church that have already been mentioned, it does not reflect well on God.

I remember meeting a young boy who was very badly behaved and had huge problems. I couldn't help wondering what his parents were like. Was his behaviour a reflection on them? In the same way, the problems of the church can appear to give a very bad impression of God. If the church is hypocritical and divided, does that reveal that God is just the same? What kind of God does the church represent?

Hypocritical?

Our perception of churches today can be very different from the Bible's concept of church. People talk about 'going to church' as if the church was a musty-smelling building with uncomfortable pews. Church to some people means an organization, with structures and regulations. However, the word 'church' originally meant just a gathering of Christians. The first churches had no buildings, elaborate authority structures or traditions. They were just communities of people from different levels of society drawn together by their belief in Jesus.

Many things may have changed in the intervening two thousand years, but one thing hasn't. Churches aren't perfect. The New Testament writers were shockingly honest about the churches they were a part of. We discover a whole variety of problems in these initial gatherings of Christians. There were schisms, popularity cults and all sorts of moral and ethical issues. Even two of the church leaders had such a sharp disagreement that for a while they couldn't work together. The very fact that the Bible exhorts Christians to bear with and forgive one another presumes that in the church people will sometimes hurt one another.

Yet this does not mean that the church is necessarily hypocritical. Hypocrisy is not the failure to be perfect, but the failure to be consistent. It is claiming one thing when the reality is totally different. If we think the church is a group of morally superior individuals, then we will be continually shocked by their ability to fail so spectacularly. However, the Bible never suggests that the church is made up of people who are better than everyone else. Actually, the truth is the opposite: Jesus said that he had not come for those who thought they were good enough, but for those who realized they were not.[2] The people most attracted to Jesus were those whose lives were clearly messed up. To be a part of Jesus' church does not mean claiming to be perfect, or even morally superior. Rather, it is realizing that we are morally bankrupt and in need of forgiveness. Churches are made up of messed-up people who have experienced God's forgiveness. Their leaders are no different.

Some people are continually shocked by news of the failings of church leaders. Yet why should this be the case? While it is sad, it is also a reminder that they are no different from anyone else. Doctors who care for the sick are just as prone to illness as anyone else. Church leaders are no different from the people they lead, as they have the same struggles and temptations. The Bible never pretends otherwise.

Peter, one of Jesus' followers, was to become a key leader of the early church. Yet on more than one occasion the Bible is shockingly honest about his failings. Not only did he publicly deny Jesus, but he needed rebuking for having a wrong attitude towards a whole group of people in the church. Churches and their leaders have no basis for claiming moral superiority. They are people who stand in need of daily forgiveness. But does this mean we should never expect people to change?

A work in progress

Some friends of mine recently bought a new house. A few weeks after they had purchased it, I went round to visit. The place was a mess. Floors were bare, plaster was falling off the walls and lights hung from exposed wires in the ceiling. Only a few rooms were even habitable. I asked them why they had bought a house in such a bad state. They looked surprised. 'You should have seen it when we moved in!' they exclaimed. 'It was a lot worse then.' They showed me photographs of rooms with piles of rubbish stacked on rotting carpets. I went to visit them again recently. The house has changed again. The work has been completed, and it now looks great.

Similarly, the church is a work in progress. It is filled with forgiven people who are being slowly changed. There is still a lot of work to be done, but there has already been real transformation. Often Christians can be unfairly judged on how they compare with the next person. It is much better to ask how they have changed from what they used to be. The question is not where they are, but where they have come from. We may be shocked that the teenager who became a Christian still uses bad language and gets angry, but if we know that a few weeks ago he was fighting and dealing in drugs, we realize that change has already happened. A couple who have become Christians may still have arguments, but that is great progress from the physical violence that used to characterize their relationship.

Sadly, there are some situations where there seems to be no evidence of change at all. Despite some people claiming on the surface to be Christians, their lives seem to be going in the opposite direction. The reality is that the direction of their lives reveals the intent of their hearts. Jesus said that a tree is known by its fruit.[3] The garden centre may have labelled it an apple tree, but if you find pears on it you can be pretty certain they got it wrong. Not everyone who claims to be a Christian is necessarily one inwardly. They may know how to say the right things on a Sunday, but the way they treat their family and their work colleagues during the week can be quite revealing. I remember one woman telling me that she would think about becoming a Christian when her husband started living like one at home.

If you are angered by hypocrisy, you are in good company. Jesus' strongest words were against such people.[4] He was not fooled by their outward shows of morality, but understood the real condition of their hearts.

Divided?

I may be slightly unusual, but I really like Tesco's. Near where I live there are at least seven of their stores I can choose from. The thing that I love about them is that they are all the same! You know what you are getting and you know they'll have it and that it will cost the same as at all the other stores.

Some people think the church should be like Tesco's. There should just be one 'brand' in every town. But the reality is that churches are a lot more like corner shops: that is, they're all different. Why are there so many churches and denominations?

Division is to be expected

If Christianity is true, then what would you expect to find? One united global organization with identical branding and beliefs? But wouldn't we be very suspicious of such uniformity? We rightly suspect cults and sects where everyone is told exactly what to believe, leaving no room for discussion.

Perhaps we might expect to find thousands of different organizations all believing different things. One of them might be right, but how could we ever know which one? What if we were to make the wrong choice? Perhaps it would be safer not even to bother.

Yet is it not more likely that we would expect to find something else? Not one uniform organization, nor 33,000 denominations with totally different beliefs, but many churches with different styles and structures, yet a core message that is essentially the same. There might be differences of opinion on certain issues and practices, but on the main points of the Bible's teaching there would be agreement. That is, in fact, what we do find. The existence of different types of church does not deny that Christian is true, but in many ways is an evidence of it.

One of the best parts of my job is that I get to travel widely, not only within Britain but also to mainland Europe. My experience of churches is that they can be very different. Some are very traditional and formal, while others are contemporary and relaxed. Some christen babies and others baptize adults. There are those where people speak in tongues and prophesy, and others which think we shouldn't. Yet all that doesn't stop them agreeing on what the Bible describes as the matters 'of first importance'[5] – Jesus' life, death and resurrection and all they achieved for us. The Bible expects that on some less important issues Christians will have differences of opinion. On these issues, the attitude we show to those we disagree with is as important as the views we hold.

Christians will have differences of opinion.

Division is not always a bad thing

It is not always a bad thing that there are several different types of church in one area. Functionally, it enables them to get on with focusing on the important issues without having to spend all their energy and time working out how to resolve practically the matters that are less important. Many churches can then still work together and support one another in the work they do.

The town in which I live has many different types of church. I have often thought that it would be brilliant if there could be only one. Idealistically, we could combine our resources and energy in one central church. Yet the reality would be quite different. Most of our energy would be spent on trying to work out how to reconcile issues that were not necessarily very important anyway.

In practice, what happens is that each church has slightly different characteristics, with some holding slightly different views on parts of the Bible from others. Yet this does not mean that many of the churches cannot work together on specific projects and events. While we recognize our differences, we can also celebrate our unity in the same core message.

Sometimes division is vital

Sometimes, however, it is right that churches should separate. When the issue at stake is the core teaching of the Bible, division is vital. If this doesn't happen, the church that is left doesn't really remain a church.

Imagine that I and a friend own a coffee shop. Each week we have a meeting to discuss business and share ideas. Sometimes my business partner suggests new flavours of coffee or types of cake that we could try. It would be totally fine to try these different ideas. But what if he thinks we should stop selling coffee and start selling flowers? Now we can't stop selling coffee and still be a coffee shop. Even with my limited business knowledge, I know that that wouldn't be possible.

Sometimes in the history of the church there have been groups and individuals who have moved so significantly far from the core teaching of Christianity that it has been right to split off from them. It is not simply a matter of style, or an issue of secondary importance that has been called into question, but the central issues themselves. That is why groups like the Jehovah's Witnesses or the Mormons are referred to as 'cults'. They may claim to be the true church, but on the basic issues of Jesus' identity and his death they have views very different from the clear teaching of the Bible.

Again, in the Bible this is not unexpected. The New Testament warns continually about false teachers who will teach a different message. Christians are warned not to associate with them. The fact that there are counterfeit churches doesn't discount the possibility of there being authentic churches. Actually, a counterfeit shows the value of the real thing. No one bothers to counterfeit a two pence piece!

Before I got a new email address I used to receive regular spam messages pretending to be from eBay. These normally asked me to enter my personal details and passwords into their counterfeit website. Why did they choose eBay and not some other company? Because eBay is successful and people usually trust it, the spammers felt they could hijack the cause and abuse people's trust.

In the same way, the church has often been hijacked and abused because people have seen that it has been successful. It is because people have often trusted and valued the church that others have tried to use it for their own selfish purposes. The presence of such counterfeit groups shows us that, while there are fakes to be avoided, there is also a reality that is good.

Round the corner from the offce where I work is a building with big red doors. Above the doors is a large sign saying 'Fire

Station'. A visitor to Bournemouth might well expect to see fire engines going in and out of it. However, while it looks like a fire station, it isn't. It used to be, but now it is a night club. It's OK for a party, but not much use in an emergency.

In a similar way, not every church that claims to be a church is one in reality. A church is not a church because it is a certain shape or size, or because the people sing songs and read from the Bible. A real church is made up of people who trust and follow the Jesus revealed in the Bible and take seriously what the Bible says about him. But does this mean they can look down on everyone else?

Judgmental?

To be judgmental about people is to think that we are better than they are. We hate judgmental attitudes! They not only put other people down, but reveal arrogance and pride that are really unpleasant.

Churches that really understand the message of the Bible will know that a judgmental attitude is inconsistent with what they believe. At the heart of the Bible is a message of forgiveness. People are not accepted by God on the basis of what they have done or how good they have been. The first step in becoming a Christian is to realize that we are no better than anyone else and in equal need of forgiveness from God.

Jesus told a story about two people who went to pray. One was a religious leader, well known for his morality and respected for his strict religious observance. The other was a tax collector, despised as a cheat and a thief. The first stood up to pray in full view of the watching crowd. He thanked God that he was better than other people, especially the tax collector, and listed his religious credentials to remind God (and the listening crowd) how worthy he was. The tax collector meanwhile stood at the back, out of view. He hung his head low, realizing that his life was a mess, and asked God to forgive him. Jesus concluded that it was the tax collector, not the religious leader, who went home accepted by God.[6]

People who have understood what it is to be forgiven by God have no basis on which to look down on other people: we are all on the same level. The PhD student is on an equal footing with the retired bin man. A lady who recently started coming to our church commented on how accepted she felt, especially by those who had been church members for years.

A friend of mine was a member of a church in Bristol. One Sunday an MP came to visit. The MP was amazed, seeing young and old working together and loving one another, and people from all areas of society united and caring for one another. He remarked, 'I spend millions of pounds trying to get people from different parts of society to get on together, and you do it for free.'

That church is not perfect. It will still have issues to deal with and disagreements to resolve. But a church full of people who have experienced grace and live in the light of it is a wonderful place to be.

What does the church tell us about God?

What kind of God does the church reveal? A messed-up, hypocritical, divided one? A God in need of forgiveness – or something else?

I did eventually meet the parents of the badly behaved boy I mentioned earlier. When I did, I felt instantly rebuked. They were nothing like what I expected. They were patient and loving and incredibly caring. I learnt later that they had adopted their child from a very difficult situation. They had been through heartache and pain as they had done their very best to love him and give him a secure home. The problems in their child did not reflect anything negative in their parenting, but quite the opposite. My initial conclusions about them had been wrong.

When we look at the church, with all its problems and difficulties, we may naturally think that it reflects a God who is also hypocritical and divided. Yet the reality is quite the opposite. The fact that God would adopt a group of people like this shows us something amazing about his character. We see his love for people who are totally unworthy. We see his patience with them, as they continue to fail and make mistakes. We see how his power is slowly changing them to become the people he wants them to be. The Bible goes on to say that the church is so loved by Jesus that it is his bride being prepared for an amazing wedding day in the future. He loves the church and gave his life for it. One day it will be finally perfected.

Until then, the church continues to reveal God's infinite wisdom, immeasurable love and continuing patience. It's a place for messed-up people to find forgiveness and acceptance and the power to change. It is a community of people who are loved by God and precious to him. He invites you to join, too.

7. PETTY, INTOLERANT AND EXCLUSIVE?

What kind of God allows only one way?

A politician is being grilled on the TV news. He is asked a straight question that requires a one-word answer. He begins to look uncomfortable and tries to avoid the issue. He is asked again, but still does not answer. It's so frustrating. I am aware that as Christians we can often appear to be the same: avoiding the issues and not answering the question.

So here is a question: do I believe that Jesus Christ is the *only* way to God and that following him is the only way we should live?

Answer: yes.

At which point, you may be thinking, 'How arrogant!' How can Christians think they are right and others are wrong? It makes God seem like the petty head teacher who sent me home from school for wearing a shirt that was the wrong shade of blue. He appears to be intolerant of perfectly good people, excluding the vast majority of the population of the world.

Christians have sometimes reinforced this view by acting as if they were better than everyone else. At other times it has seemed as though being a Christian means coming from a certain culture or fitting in with a particular class of society. All of this can seem pretty arrogant. But could it be that we have misunderstood the issues.

Is God petty?

I remember when I first visited the United States and watched a game of American football. Having been brought up watching rugby each week, I figured that it must be about the same. After all, the ball was a similar shape, and the pitch was about the same size, with goal posts at each end. How wrong I was! In this game they tackled you even if you didn't have the ball. You could 'forward pass' as much as you liked, and 'touchdowns' didn't even involve touching the ball down. (I still can't figure that one out!) Some people understand differences in religion in a similar way.

As we saw earlier, it is often suggested that all religions are really the same: like different brands of baked beans, they may have different packaging, but the contents are perceived to be pretty much identical. Religion is often reduced to three main ingredients:

- *Thinking*: agreeing to certain ideas and philosophies about life
- *Feeling*: having a certain type of spiritual experience
- *Doing*: obeying a set of rules about how to live, or maintaining a specific lifestyle.

If we think of religion in this way, it is not hard to see why we would think of God as being petty. Is it right to reject someone simply on the basis of their philosophy or ideas? Should someone who has had a different experience of spirituality be told that it is not authentic? How can one certain lifestyle be better or more deserving of God's acceptance than another?

However, thinking in this way is to misunderstand what it means to be a Christian. The heart of the Bible's message is not that we simply need to *think*, *feel* or *act* differently. Our basic problem is much deeper than our minds, emotions and actions. The Bible reveals that our real need is to *be* different people. Real Christianity is about *being* before it is about *thinking*, *feeling* or *doing*. To understand this, we need to take a step back and look at the big picture.

The world as it was

The world we live in today is not the same as the one God originally created. The Bible records that everything that God made was 'very good'[1] – from snow-capped mountains to white sandy beaches. Families and friendships, as well as love, sex and marriage, were all his creations and were all described as good. It was a perfect set-up where people had an unspoilt relationship with God, with each other and with the world around them.

The world as it is

We can still see something of this original goodness in our world. When we enjoy the beauty of the Rocky Mountains or a Mediterranean beach, or experience the love of family and the joy of friendship, then we appreciate something of God's good world. But other experiences in life tell us that something has gone wrong. Our lives are a mixture of joys and sorrows, elation and despair. Families break down, friends fall out. Societies struggle with the problems of crime and disorder. Those we trust can let us down, and people we love die. As we have seen, even the environment has been affected: the effects of global warming threaten whole regions of the world. Something has gone wrong.

This is because, rather than live in relationship with God, humanity has turned its back on its Creator. By nature each of us goes our own way rather than God's. Rather than live under God's good rule we make up our own, and then wonder why the world doesn't work the way it should. At some level, we all spoil the world. The perfect relationships that we were created to enjoy have been ruined. As well as being cut off from God, we find our human relationships are spoilt and damaged, often by our own selfishness. Even our relationship with the world around us is affected.

The world as it will be

The great news of the Bible is that God has done something about the mess in our world. He has set a date when he will make 'a new heaven and a new earth'.[2] All that currently spoils this world will be removed, and perfect relationships will be restored. It will be a place where there is 'no more death or mourning or crying or pain'.[3] It is a fantastic picture of the kind of world that we would all want to be a part of: all the enjoyment of this world, but with all that ruins it taken away.

As we saw in chapter 4, it is important not to see this new world as a fluffy cloudlike experience of endless choir practice. The Bible describes it as a real, touchable, physical creation. A perfect place, with mountains to ski over and waves to surf, valleys to walk through and lakes to swim in, food to eat and wine to drink, art to appreciate and music to play and compose; a place to enjoy friends and families, love and acceptance. Yet what won't be there is also significant. No need for hospitals, because there will be no sickness. No need for tissues, because there will be no tears. No need for funerals, because there will be no death. No selfishness or sin, and no divorce and distrust. An amazing world.

The problem

For us, there is only one problem with this new world. We wouldn't fit in. How can I live in a world where there is no crying or pain, when I can cause both of these reactions in others by my selfish actions and cutting words? We would spoil such a perfect world. The problem with our world is not in some distant country, but in our hearts. It is *who* we are that is the problem.

In the Coldplay song 'Clocks', Chris Martin asks the question 'Am I part of the cure or am I part of the disease?' We may like to think that we are the answer to the world's problems, but experience shows that we are part of the problem. That is why a religion that simply emphasizes a different way of *thinking*, *feeling* and *doing* is not enough. No amount of intellectual thought, spiritual experience, or attempts at good behaviour can solve the problem. We need to be different. We need to change.

There was a deeply religious man called Nicodemus who once came to speak to Jesus at night. He was one of the most respected members of his society. He was the first-century equivalent of a university professor, the Archbishop of Canterbury and a senior politician all rolled into one. In the minds of many, if anyone was right before God then this man was. But rather than commend him for his religious credentials, Jesus said to him, 'You must be born again.'[4] What exactly was Jesus saying?

A new start

Imagine I decide that I would quite like to play football for Manchester United. I ring up the club and ask for a trial. They kindly agree, and so I pack my football boots and head north. When I get there, I run out onto the training ground to show them what I am made of. After a woeful few minutes of missed tackles, sliced kicks and painful attempts at headers, the trial is bought to an end.

One of the coaches calls me over to tell me what he thinks. 'Thank you for coming today,' he says politely. At this I get my hopes up, but then he continues: 'I just want you to know that after today's performance your only real hope of playing for us is if you were to be born again!'

What is he trying to say? That I am pretty good and I just need to try a bit harder? Perhaps I need to put in some more practice? Not at all! He is really saying, 'Michael, you are too fat and already too old. You have no coordination and two left feet. You have no natural ability and no hope of ever gaining it. Your only hope of joining our club is if you were to be born again, but this time as someone who is fitter and faster and has at least a little bit of coordination.'[5]

Jesus says we need to be born again. We need a completely new start. God is not being petty. It is just that other ways don't deal with the real problem of our hearts. This is much deeper than what we think, how we feel, or what we do. The problem lies in who we are. As a virus infects a computer, so our very natures are infected by sin. No matter how hard we try, we will never be the people we were designed to be. We need more than human effort; we need a divine miracle. The Bible describes someone who has become a Christian as 'a new creation; the old has gone, the new has come!'[6]

Is God intolerant?

Towards the end of his time as British Prime Minister, Tony Blair stated that tolerance is 'what makes Britain', and that we must be ready to defend this attitude.[7] Less than two weeks later, during her annual Christmas Day speech, the Queen said, 'I believe tolerance and fair play remain strong British values.'[8]

Tolerance has certainly become one of the buzz words of our generation. It seems to have become a value that we are not allowed to question. We must be tolerant of everyone, no matter what. While it is easy to see why this has happened, is it always such a good thing?

Tolerant of whom?

To what degree are we to be tolerant and is there a limit to it? Should we be tolerant of everyone, no matter what their beliefs or practices? For instance, are we to tolerate an Ian Huntley, convicted of murdering two pupils of the school where he was caretaker? What about a Harold Shipman, who used his position as a GP to murder vulnerable women? Should we tolerate an Adolf Hitler or a Pol Pot?

To tolerate such people would surely show that we didn't care too much about what they did. Tolerating gives the impression that we are willing to overlook something and not care too much about it. But most of us *do* care. We have a problem with a man who kills schoolchildren, or a dictator who is responsible for the deaths of six million Jews. We don't want to tolerate people like that. Neither does God. The good news is that God does not tolerate evil. He does not overlook it, or say that it doesn't matter very much. Evil and injustice do matter.

But where does that leave us? We may not kill people with a gun, but we can assassinate their reputations with words. We may not abuse children, but by our greed we can selfishly live in luxury while others suffer from a lack of basic necessities. Should God be tolerant of my selfishness, greed and gossip? Does he care about the person cut down by my harsh words? God cannot just look at my life and say that what I do doesn't matter. It does.

Better than tolerant

The Bible never describes God as being tolerant. Instead, he is characterized by something much better: forgiveness. Tolerance would mean that God doesn't care, but his forgiveness shows us that he does. He cares about evil and must deal with it. But he also cares about us, who are all too capable of doing evil.

Forgiveness is very different from tolerance. It's the difference between saying to someone who has hurt you, 'It's OK,' or 'I forgive you.' To say 'It's OK' suggests that it wasn't really a big issue. But what if it was a big issue? In that case, forgiveness is better. In forgiving, we are saying that it wasn't OK, but we are willing to deal with the offence and accept the person.

Our only hope with God is that he can provide a way by which we can be accepted and forgiven by him. God cannot look at the wrong of our lives and say 'It's OK,' but he can say 'I forgive you.'

Taking the initiative

Imagine that, one Saturday, I and three friends decide to travel to London. In the absence of anything better to do, we decide that we would quite like to go to Buckingham Palace and meet the Queen. With no offcial invitation and a blatant disregard for the security system, we plan our entrance.

One of us decides to parachute into the gardens at the rear of the palace. He jumps out of the plane at 10,000 feet and starts to descend on the palace. Another decides to burrow from Green Park into the Palace grounds. The sporty one decides he will simply try to outrun the guards when they open up the gates for the postman, while I opt for the 'Prince Charles fancy dress kit'.

Now, even if we were to make it into the Palace grounds and by some massive failure of the security services arrive in the presence of Her Majesty, it is almost certain that none of us would remain there very long! We are free to try our own ways of getting inside, but the only way that will ever work is for her to take the initiative. She must invite us inside.

The amazing news of the Bible is that God has taken the initiative to make it possible for people like us to be accepted by him. The sin in our own hearts matters and must be dealt with. We don't deserve to stand in his presence or be accepted by him. But God himself, through the death of Jesus in our place, has taken the punishment we deserve for all the wrong of our lives and made acceptance possible.

The death of Jesus shows us how intolerant of evil God is. Evil must be punished, but on the cross we find Jesus taking it in our place. The rightful and just anger of God at every child abuser, murderer and rapist, as well his anger at every gossip, liar and selfish person, was poured out on Jesus. God couldn't overlook these things, or say that they didn't matter, because they do.

The death of Jesus also shows us how much God loves us. He was willing to take the initiative, deal with our problem and make it possible for us to be forgiven and made new. God is intolerant of evil, yet through what he has done he can also be forgiving. God doesn't look at us and say, 'It's OK,' but much better, he can say, 'I forgive you.' Tolerance will never change us, but forgiveness will. Forgiveness is the basis from which we can become the people that we were meant to be.

Is God exclusive?

Yes . . . and no! I'm not meaning to sound like an indecisive politician, but it really depends on what we mean by 'exclusive'.

If by 'exclusive' we mean that the death and resurrection of Jesus is the only way to get to God and be right with him, then yes, he is. No other philosophy or system of religion deals with the real problem of the human heart or offers the forgiveness that Jesus brings.

However, if by 'exclusive' we mean that this message is just for certain people who were brought up in Christian families or in a Western country, then no. The message of the Bible, from beginning to end, far from being exclusive, is actually a very inclusive one. Consider the following:

- Just twelve chapters into the Bible, God called Abraham to be the father of the nation of Israel. God promised that through Abraham 'all peoples on earth will be blessed'.[9] God's plan was always bigger than one family or nation.
- All through the Old Testament we read about people from other nations and cultures becoming part of God's people. The family tree of Jesus includes several foreigners, among them a widow and a prostitute.
- When Jesus was born, the angels announced that this was 'good news of great joy that will be for *all* the people'.[10] Among the first people to meet Jesus were a group of working-class shepherds and several high-powered astrologers (probably from present-day Iraq).
- Jesus went out of his way to meet a woman from a different religious and cultural background. When she told her neighbours what had happened, and they had heard Jesus for themselves, they declared that he was the 'Saviour of the world'.[11]

- Jesus gave his disciples instructions that they were to take this good news 'to the ends of the earth'.[12] The rest of the Bible story is an outworking of that command, as people from Africa, Asia and Europe and from all sorts of social and religious backgrounds receive the good news about Jesus.
- The last book of the Bible looks forward to a day in the future when those from 'every nation, tribe, people and language'[13] will come to worship Jesus.

The Bible shows that rather than being exclusive, God's rescue mission can include all. No one needs to be excluded. All who are willing to turn to Jesus and trust him to forgive them are accepted by God.

I think the church I am part of is a little reflection of the inclusiveness of God. On any given Sunday, along with Europeans, we have people from Asia, North and South America and Africa. There are young and old, and others in between. Some are quite posh, with accents to match, while others are not. Some were brought up in Christian families, others in homes where they would have never even have heard of Jesus. A few have high-powered jobs selling aeroplanes and houses, while others stack shelves at Asda or are studying at university. Yet all of them have one thing in common: they have come to trust in Jesus and have experienced his forgiveness.

The fact that there is only one way doesn't mean that we are not free to *try* to get to God in different ways. But doing so would be like trying to swim the Atlantic Ocean when you've already been offered a free plane ticket!

Why would God have only one way? Not because he is petty. Our problem runs deeper than what we think or how we feel. We need to be changed to become new people. God is not tolerant of evil, but, far more wonderfully, he is able to forgive. Far from being exclusive to a few, this great news is open to everyone, including you.

8. REPRESSIVE, RESTRICTIVE AND RESTRAINING?

What kind of God would limit my sexuality?

'So you're a Christian, then?' my colleague asked, as we folded clothes in the Edinburgh shop where we both worked. 'So that basically means you don't drink, you don't smoke and you don't have sex before marriage, right?'

Many people's perception of God is that he is anti-sex. Why else would he place so many restrictions on our enjoyment of it? Isn't God's blueprint for sex restrictive and repressive?

Christians through the ages have often contributed to this idea. Origen, a church leader in the second century, said: 'Adam did not have sexual knowledge of his wife Eve until after the Fall. If it had not been for the Fall, the human race would likely have been propagated in some very mysterious or angelic manner without sex and therefore sin.'[1] Origen certainly practised what he preached – he castrated himself.

Things didn't get much better in the Middle Ages. Yves of Chartres taught that Christians should abstain from sex on five out of seven days of the week: 'Thursdays in memory of the arrest of our Lord, on Fridays in honour of his death, Saturdays in honour of the Virgin Mary, on Sundays in commemoration of the resurrection, and on Mondays out of respect for the faithfully departed.'[2] I guess a lot of Christians are glad that they don't live in the Middle Ages. In those days it was not a case of 'Thank God it's Friday', but rather 'Thank God it's Tuesday'!

Even today, some Christians seem to give the impression that God is against sex. Once when I was speaking at a Christian youth meeting, I happened to mention the word 'sex' in my talk. One of the youth leaders saw me afterwards and suggested I shouldn't use the 's' word, particularly in front of young people!

Yet more serious is the suggestion that God is homophobic. Why would he stop certain people from being able to enjoy sexual fulfilment? Christians are often seen as being anti-gay, perhaps because they seem to get media attention only when they are protesting against legislation regarding homosexuality. In an advanced and tolerant society that accepts people regardless of gender, race and skin colour, why should people be rejected because of their sexual orientation? Surely this is bigoted and prejudiced?

Sadly, Christians have sometimes not helped in changing this stereotype. Often this is because they fail to distinguish between homosexuality in orientation and in practice; yet this is an important distinction to make. All too frequently, Christians have condemned homosexuality while showing little or no understanding of or compassion for those for whom this is an issue. Sometimes it has been isolated as a worse sin than all others: one for which there is almost no forgiveness. Worse still is the presence of groups like 'God hates fags', who seem to blame every national catastrophe on the homosexual community.

If you have ever been on the receiving end of such attitudes, then I am sorry. There should be no place for homophobia and prejudice of this sort in the Christian church, and when, sadly, it is present, it needs to be repented of.

So why would a good God be so repressive and limiting in our enjoyment of sex? If God has our best interests at heart, why does it appear that he is so determined to spoil our fun? What do we discover about God's attitude to sex in the Bible?

Sex is great

I was on the panel of a 'Grill a Christian' event at one university. Students had been invited to come and ask us any questions they liked about God and Christianity. As nearly always happens, a question about sex came up. The questioner wanted our opinion on just about every type of sexual behaviour that you could think of. Several members of the panel had given their opinions before it came to me. I decided that a brief answer was best, so I simply stated, 'God thinks sex is great. After all, it was his idea!' I could see the surprise on people's faces. That was not what they were expecting to hear.

Yet that is what the Bible teaches. Sex, in contrast to Origen's teaching, was not the result of sin. It was part of God's original creation. God made humans sexual beings: not just with the ability to have sex, but to enjoy it as well. It would seem that humans have a lot more fun, when it comes to sex, than the rest of the animal kingdom. When God made the world, he made sex. Along with everything else he made, he declared that it was 'very good'.[3]

God was neither shocked nor surprised when Adam and Eve discovered the joy of sex. He didn't look on and wonder, 'Whatever are they getting up to?!' Sex was one of his gifts to humanity, and he created it for us to enjoy. There is a whole book of the Bible, the Song of Songs, which celebrates the joy and intimacy of sex. In fact, it is so explicit that Jewish children under the age of sixteen were not allowed to read it! In the New Testament, the apostle Paul even warns Christian couples not to get so super-spiritual that they stop having sex.[4]

God was neither shocked nor surprised when Adam and Eve discovered the joy of sex.

So why the limitations?

The Bible is clear that sexuality was designed to be expressed in a certain context. At the beginning of the Bible, God says: 'A man will leave his father and mother and be united to his wife [marriage], and they will become one flesh [sex].'[5] Yet this is not just the teaching of the Old Testament. It is also reiterated by Jesus.[6] The Bible's blueprint for sex is that it is to be between two people of the opposite sex in a marriage relationship. That means that, when it comes to sex, the Bible's teaching is a challenge to everyone, whatever situation they are in.

If sex is so good, why would God restrict our enjoyment of it and put it only within the context of marriage? Isn't it better to get as much of it as possible, with as many partners as possible, in whatever way we want it?

Things work best in the way they were designed

Recently I got a new phone. The advert claimed that it could do just about anything. I was excited about seeing if it really was as good as they made out. As with most new purchases that I make, I didn't want to bother with the instruction manual. At 200 pages, I thought, it was far too long even to look at. I wanted to get on and enjoy the phone. Unfortunately, I was soon to discover that reading the instruction manual would have been a good idea. Even my brother, who is pretty good at technological gadgets, couldn't figure it out. Several hours of frustration later, I succumbed to opening the manual and discovering how the thing actually worked. The manufacturers were the best people to show me how it should be used.

If human beings are designed by God, this will have implications for the way we think about sex. Sexual pleasure was not just some accident of evolution, but part of God's plan. It would be obvious to expect, therefore, that God might have something to say about it. The Bible is not a detailed instruction manual on sex, but it does give a blueprint for its use that is for both our protection and our long-term joy.

Good things are to be valued

The tag line for Rolo chocolates asked the question 'Who would you share your last Rolo with?' In other words, you should think carefully before you give it away. It is not because their chocolates are so tasteless, unpalatable and disgusting that you wouldn't want to share them with anyone. What they are trying communicate is that their chocolates are so amazing, tasty and enjoyable that you should value them.

We treat carefully the things that we value. If something is very precious, you think twice about who you give it to. When it comes to sex, it is because it is good and precious that God places restrictions upon it. The message is not that sex is bad. In fact it is quite the opposite. Sex is good and precious, and because of this we should value it. The answer is to value it more, not less. The way to really enjoyable and satisfying sex is a committed relationship: a relationship where both sides are committed to each other and where there is no continual fear of rejection.

Contrary to popular opinion, evidence[7] shows that couples who don't live together before marriage are much more likely to stay together in the long term than those who do. Neither is marriage boring. Surveys show that married couples find sex more physically and emotionally satisfying and enjoy it more regularly than their unmarried counterparts.[8]

If you went sky diving, the parachute would not be there to restrict your fun. It would be there to keep you safe. Freedom from a parachute might appear to make the jump more fun, but it would also ensure it was your last. God's instructions on sex are there to protect us and enable us to enjoy it in the long term. They are not arbitrary and restrictive, but loving and wise.

When we reject God's blueprint for sex, we don't merely miss out on the best way to enjoy it, we also cause hurt to ourselves and to others. Sexual intimacy is like the glue that holds a relationship together. When two people have shared with each other in such an intimate way, deep hurts and scars are left. The Bible teaches that 'he who sins sexually sins against his own body'.[9] Sexual sin hurts us, as well as others.

Following God's blueprint for sex is not the easiest way to live. At times it will be a struggle against our own basic desires. Whatever our situation, living life God's way will mean going against the flow of society and sometimes being ridiculed by others. But, while it is not easy, God's way is still the best way to enjoy sex.

Sex is not everything

It may be that after reading this far, you are thinking, 'Well, that is OK for those who are married. But what about those who are not? Do they miss out on the best life has to offer?'

The problem with British society is that it would appear that sex is the ultimate thing. Websites, films and advertisements are full of it. The message communicated is that sex is everything, and to miss out on sex is to miss out on life. Sex has become a god that we worship and the main source of our identity. If sex is the ultimate thing in life, to miss out on it (for whatever reason) is to miss out on life itself.

Sex shouldn't be our god

Treating sex as a kind of god is nothing new. People did the same in the times when the Bible was written. In the context of a passage that teaches about sex, the Bible says that people have 'exchanged the truth of God for a lie, and worshipped and served created things rather than the Creator'.[10] People take a good thing and make it everything. They enjoy the gift, but end up worshipping it and not the giver.

That kind of attitude is what the Bible calls sin. Taking God's gifts, but rejecting God the giver. It is like a child at Christmas who is so engrossed with a new present that he never says 'Thank you' to the person who gave it.

Making sex into a god is also disastrous for our enjoyment of it. Whatever we expect to give us *ultimate joy* and satisfaction functionally becomes our god. It becomes the thing that gives our lives meaning. Sex was never designed to give ultimate joy and satisfaction. Sexual intimacy in marriage is a great thing, but it was always designed to point us towards something even better.

In the Bible, the intimacy of a marriage relationship is used to illustrate the kind of relationship that God wants with people.[11] Sex is great, but even at its best it is just a shadow of the most amazing and satisfying relationship that God will one day have with his people. To move away from God's blueprint for sex is to miss the even greater significance of what it points towards. Looking for ultimate joy and satisfaction in sex will inevitably lead to disappointment, frustration and even addiction, as we look for the elusive experience that we will never find.

Sex should not be the main source of our identity

If sex is the main source of our identity, then expressing our sexuality is an essential part of being who we are. Not to have sex is not really to be yourself. There are lots of people who, for whatever reason, are not in a sexual relationship. Are they not complete until they find a sexual partner?

The teaching of the Bible is that we don't need sex to be a whole person. It is part of what it means to be human, but not everything. Sexuality can be properly expressed whatever our circumstances. A single lad doesn't need to be in a sexual relationship to express his masculinity. To be truly human, what we really need is to know God. We were created in God's image to know and enjoy him. We are not truly ourselves until we experience this. Our identity is to be found in the God who made us and loves us. Jesus said eternal life was having a relationship with the God of the universe.[12] You can miss out on sex and still be a whole person, but without a relationship with God you will never know what it means to be truly human.

How can we know God?

As you have read this, you may well be acutely aware of your own failure to live according to God's design. At some level we have all failed. We have hurt others, disappointed ourselves and rejected God by living our own way in many areas of life, including sex. No one has the right to point the finger; none of us is the person we should be.

The great news is that Jesus didn't come to condemn but to save us. John, one of his followers, wrote: 'If we confess our sins, he is faithful and just and will forgive us our sins and purify us from all unrighteousness.'[13] Jesus came so that we could know forgiveness. As he died on the cross, he took the guilt and shame of all our sin. He experienced the shame of every wrong choice and selfish motive. He took what we deserve, so that we could be accepted by God. Whatever we have done, however we have failed, we can know forgiveness and be made clean on the inside. We can have a completely fresh start.

To those who have been forgiven, Jesus also brings real life. Jesus said, 'I have come that they may have life, and have it to the full.'[14] Following Jesus doesn't mean missing out on life, but finding real life. Jesus says that following him will mean dying to our own way of living, but it also means discovering his new way of living.

God is not out to limit our fun, nor is his blueprint for sex repressive. Rather, in his great love and wisdom, he has revealed how his good gift is best enjoyed. Sex is great, but it is not the most important thing in life. Rather, it points us forward to the ultimate thing: a relationship with God himself. Only in him can we find ultimate joy and satisfaction.

9. CONDEMNING, UNJUST AND ARBITRARY?

What kind of God sends sincere people to hell?

A few years ago I visited Rome. Although I was there for only two days, I tried to fit in as many of the sights as possible. One of the highlights of the whole trip was my visit to the Sistine Chapel. It took Michelangelo four years to paint the ceiling, and at one stage I thought it might take me about as long to get in. Yet, once inside, I knew it had been worth the wait.

It is not only the ceiling that is impressive. As you look towards the altar at the far end of the chapel, you see another of Michelangelo's works, *The Last Judgment*. At the top of the picture you see depictions of the saints rising to paradise. In the centre is Christ the judge, and beneath are the condemned descending into a horrific portrayal of hell. It is an impressive work of art that certainly grabs your attention. Yet I found that the longer I looked at it, the more my appreciation of the art was replaced by something deeper: the shocked realization of what the painting represents. The image of human beings descending to physical torture and pain is one that many find repulsive and appalling. This was not merely a painting. This is what people believe actually happens.

The whole question of hell is hugely emotive and horrific to contemplate. The caricatured medieval picture of a God who delights in throwing people into a fiery lake gives us huge emotional problems. How could a good God send people to such a place?

Christians have sometimes been sadly insensitive when it comes to this issue. People can often wonder whether Christians have normal human emotions. The preacher who stands on a street corner and seems glibly to tell people of their dire eternal destiny does very little to help us understand the concept of hell.

I remember being shocked at the technique of an enthusiastic – but rather tactless – lad who was trying to persuade someone to become a Christian. He grabbed a cigarette lighter and held the naked flame next to the hand of the other person. When they screamed in pain he said, 'If you thought that was painful, you wouldn't like hell. The fire never goes out there!'

A slightly more advanced, but equally worrying technique is used by one group in the United States. The 'Hell House' is a dramatized presentation of the horrors of hell for children. The website states: 'This sizzling evangelism event is designed to capture the attention of our *sight and sound* culture!' It's not hard to see why people would be appalled at such methods being used to try to persuade children to 'convert'.

Our problem is that hell is not the invention of medieval painters or religious fanatics. The ideas of hell and judgment are found throughout the Bible's teaching – not only in the Old Testament, but in the New Testament as well. And it's not just in the writings of the early Christians, but most of all in Jesus' own words. He describes hell as a place of agony and torment,[1] where the 'worm does not die, and the fire is not quenched',[2] a place of 'weeping and gnashing of teeth',[3] an 'eternal fire'.[4]

How can a good, loving and just God allow a place like hell? We struggle with the concept of it, wondering how God could deliberately create such a place and send people there. Doesn't this reveal an evil, vindictive and unjust God? This is a big issue, and an emotionally charged one, for those who are already Christians as well as those who are not.

How can a good, loving and just God allow a place like hell?

Yet the Bible shows us that, although hell is real, it is not a contradiction to God's goodness. It is because God is good, just and loving that there is a hell. Now, I guess that at this point you may be scratching your head and wondering whether the last sentence was wrongly phrased. Surely there must be a mistake? How could hell tell us about God's goodness, love and justice?

A longing for justice

Recently, while visiting my parents, I took the opportunity to go and watch a rugby match (as Leicester is home to the best team in Europe!). During the second half, the referee (who frequently seems to be employed by the opposition) didn't see an offence by the opposition that would have resulted in a penalty. I felt angered that justice had not been done, and – along with thousands of others – told him so! There is a natural feeling of indignation when justice is not done. But that was just a rugby match. How much greater is the sense of anger when it is not a rugby match but human lives that are at stake?

When the teenager Steven Lawrence was murdered during a racially motivated attack, the police were almost certain who was responsible. Yet years later, because of a legal technicality, no one has ever been convicted of his murder. His killers still walk free. Something inside us is angered. Justice has not been done and evil has not been punished.

This is just one individual case among thousands. How many more court cases have happened where justice has not been done? What about the six million Jews killed during the Second World War – was justice ever done? What about the million Kurds killed in Iraq under an evil dictatorship – was the hanging of Saddam Hussein really justice?

Something in our hearts longs for justice to be done and is angered when it isn't. We feel the need for evil to be punished and wrongs to be put right. The good news of the Bible is that God is perfectly righteous and just and will ensure that the right thing is ultimately done. Justice will be accomplished. He does not turn a blind eye to the injustices of this world and he does not tolerate evil. Rather, he is angered by the wickedness of this world and will do something about it.

A right kind of anger

We don't always think of anger as a good thing. We often associate it with a sudden loss of temper. One of my course mates at college borrowed a computer to type up his dissertation. As he neared completion, the computer 'crashed', losing weeks of his work in the process. In his anger he picked up the machine and threw it out of the first-floor window. Thankfully, there was no one walking below at the time, but, needless to say, it didn't fix the problem!

God's anger is very different. It is not a sudden loss of temper but a controlled, settled reaction to all that is wrong. We too can feel that right kind of anger when we look at the injustices and evil on the news each day. The Bible says that ultimately God's anger will be expressed on 'the day of God's wrath, when his righteous judgment will be revealed'.[5] If we are grieved by evil, we can know that he is, too. If we are concerned for justice, he is far more so. God cares when his good world is ruined and people that he loves are hurt by the selfishness and sin of others.

The apostle Paul, one of the leaders of the early church, was once preaching to a group of intellectuals in the city of Athens. He finished his sermon by declaring that God 'has set a day when he will judge the world with justice by the man he has appointed. He has given proof of this to all men by raising him [Jesus] from the dead.'[6] Although the story of the world is so often of injustice reigning, there will be a day of justice in the future. The message of the Bible is that God will one day ensure that justice is done. Every wrong will be put right, every evil will be punished, every injustice overturned.

The fact that God is angry about sin and will bring about justice by setting a day of judgment is not a reflection of anything negative in his character. It is rather a demonstration of his goodness. The justice of God flows from his goodness. It would be evil of God *not* to judge. What kind of God would stand by and say that it doesn't matter? What would it say about God if at the end he turns to an Adolf Hitler and says that it doesn't matter? This does not mean that hell is any less terrible to contemplate. But the alternative is even worse: a God who doesn't care about evil or justice. The Bible says that God is good and will ensure that justice is one day done.

> *The justice of God flows from his goodness.*

What about 'good' people?

Of course, to talk like this is not too uncomfortable. Ultimately, we might quite like the idea of people getting what they deserve. There will always be evil and dangerous people out there, but it is easy to conclude that we are in no way like them.

When the mass murderer Myra Hindley died, the Scottish author Ian Rankin wrote an illuminating article on the subject of evil. He concluded by saying:

> We prefer to demonize certain people. Put evil in a world of monsters, because it prevents us confronting the fact that these people are just like us, the people next door. It lets us off the hook.[7]

It's scary to realize that every human heart is capable of evil and that, given the right circumstances, we might do exactly the same as those we so often despise.

When Jesus identified the source of evil he (in effect) explained that it was not limited to North Korea or a prison cell.

> What comes out of a man is what makes him 'unclean'. For from within, out of men's hearts, come evil thoughts, sexual immorality, theft, murder, adultery, greed, malice, deceit, lewdness, envy, slander, arrogance and folly. All these evils come from inside and make a man 'unclean'.[8]

What makes that list so worrying is that it combines things that we would not even consider with things that we wouldn't think twice about.

I don't seem to get on very well when it comes to airport security scanners. On one occasion I had successfully passed the metal detectors, only to discover that my bag had been stopped in the x-ray machine. When it eventually appeared it was hastily picked up by an offcial-looking lady, who began to search it.

The first item out was my Bible. At this point I was tempted to feel quite self-righteous. The next item was slightly more embarrassing: the autobiography of Simon Cowell. Without changing her very professional expression, she neatly placed it, along with the Bible, on a large table in full view of everyone else. Bit by bit, the contents of my bag were displayed: some papers, my phone, a packed lunch.

Suddenly a terrible realization took hold of me: it occurred to me that even *I* wasn't sure what was at the bottom of my bag! Things had gone in and had never come out. It was like a black hole. I looked up just in time to see her pull out a pair of underpants and place them on the table; then a smelly sock, a half-eaten banana, an apple core and what seemed like half of Bournemouth beach. All the items were placed on the table for everyone to see. Members of the public streamed by with bemused looks on their faces. My face had gone very red!

Finally they discovered the offending article: a screwdriver, which in the end they allowed me to keep. As I repacked my bag and walked away, I reflected. What if God were to do the same with the contents of our lives? What if all our thoughts, actions and words were displayed for all to see? There would certainly be some things to be proud of, but there would be plenty to be ashamed of, too.

Yet God does see it all, and he is not fooled. One day, the contents of our lives will be laid bare. None of us is the person we should be. It's not only the things that we have done, but what we have failed to do; not only our actions, but our words and attitudes. All of our lives are revealed and open to God.

We want him to punish the sins of others – but to be just; he must also deal with us.

Is it that serious?

If a shoplifter were sentenced to life imprisonment, we would feel that the punishment far outweighed the crime committed. That in itself would be an injustice. In the same way, we may think that God is unfair. Punishing our sin with hell may seem out of proportion. We may not be innocent, but do we feel that we deserve hell? After all, is our sin really that serious? The Bible says that what makes our sin serious is not so much what we do, but who it is against.

Imagine that, while driving home, I recklessly swerve across the road and run over a snail. No big deal (unless you are a conservationist with a passion for rare snails). But what if I hit a rabbit? That's not so good. A dog would be worse, not only because there is now a dent in my bumper, but also because I am legally obliged to stop. But if I hit a person, this is far more serious. It is who (or what) I have hit that determines the seriousness of the crime.

Sin is serious because it is ultimately not against people but against God himself. So when King David in the Old Testament committed both adultery and murder, he confessed to God that 'Against you, you only, have I sinned and done what is evil in your sight.'[9] When we sin, we don't just do things that we know to be wrong and that hurt other people, but we declare our independence from God by deliberately living life our way rather than God's. We reject his rightful and loving rule over us by making up our own rules.

Such an attitude has massive implications. The seriousness of our sin is directly related to the greatness of God. If God were just some small local deity, then ignoring him might not be that serious. But he isn't. The Bible reveals an eternal God who created everything and is above all things, so rejecting him is far more serious.

The result of our independence from God is that God gives us what, in effect, we ask for. If we live our lives without God, wanting to go our own way, then he will let us spend eternity apart from him. Heaven is a place where God lives, and it would seem strange if, after living a life of independence from him, we should want to be with him.

One of Jesus' parables helps us to understand this. He tells a story about a rich man who ends up in hell.[10] As he realizes the awfulness of his situation he asks for help from Abraham. He pleads with him for relief from the pain he feels, and he wants someone to go back and warn his brothers of the danger they too are in. Yet it is what he doesn't say that is most revealing. Not once does he ask to be taken out of hell. For hell is the consequence of the path that we have already taken – a life of independence from God.

What makes hell, hell?

A student once said to me, 'Well I think I'd enjoy hell – I haven't needed God yet in this life, and besides, I will be with my friends.' To some, hell seems like a really great party where we finally gain independence from all restraints of authority. It can seem quite attractive by comparison with the idea of eternal choir practice in heaven. To think this way is to misunderstand what the Bible says about hell.

It is not just a separation from God, but also from his goodness. In this world, whether we believe in God or not, we still enjoy many of the good things that he gives us. Friendship, love, creativity, beauty, sex, food, family, art, sport and music are just some of his gifts.

While it may be true that the Bible often uses pictorial language to describe hell, this is surely descriptive of something awful and to be avoided at all costs. Separation from God means separation from all his goodness. Hell is not a never-ending party. It is the terrible consequence of living life our way and rejecting the God who made us.

Patient and loving

Hell exists because God is righteous and justice must be done. Yet the idea of a God who secretly looks forward to casting people into hell is in complete contradiction to what the Bible says about him. One of the Bible writers put it this way: 'He [God] is patient with you, not wanting anyone to perish, but everyone to come to repentance.'[11] Far from wanting people to end up in hell, God longs for people to avoid it. Every day that judgment is delayed is a sign of his patience with a world in rebellion against him. Throughout the Bible, we see a God who is patient with people.

In fact, not only does God not want people to go to hell, he has done everything possible so that we might not have to. One of the most famous verses in the Bible says: 'God so loved the world that he gave his one and only Son, that whoever believes in him shall not perish but have eternal life.'[12]

God gave his Son to die. He was born to die. On the cross, as Jesus suffered, he experienced more than physical pain – he experienced hell. As we shall see in the next chapter, as he died Jesus faced separation from his own Father. He faced the rejection that we deserve. He willingly took what we deserve, so that we don't have to.

Our sin and rebellion against God have massive and eternal consequences, but we have a choice. Either we pay for it in hell, or Jesus pays for it on our behalf on the cross. Whether we pay or he does, someone must, because justice must be done.

There is a place called hell because God in his goodness will ensure that justice is done and evil is punished. No amount of sincerity or human effort can make up for the fact that, to varying degrees, we all deserve God's punishment. But God does not want anyone to go there. In his love he has done everything possible so that we don't have to. The only way to hell is to trample over the cross

The only way to hell is to trample over the cross of Jesus, disregard what God has done and keep going our own way.

of Jesus, disregard what God has done and keep going our own way.

Not just fire insurance . . .

We shouldn't think that becoming a Christian is just about avoiding hell, though. Christianity is not like taking out fire insurance 'just in case'. Trusting in Jesus means coming into a relationship with God, and that can begin right now. It is about discovering the reason why we were born and experiencing the life for which we were created. Ultimately, Christians can look forward to a world made new, with all that has ruined this world taken away.

What kind of God does the Bible show us? Far from condemning, unjust and arbitrary, the God of the Bible is perfectly just and infinitely loving. His justice is an expression of his love and not in contradiction to it. While our rejection of God is infinitely serious, he has done everything possible to rescue people from it.

10. 'VICIOUS, SADOMASOCHISTIC AND REPELLENT'?[1]

What kind of God would send his Son to die?

I can't stand the thought of execution. Whether or not the death penalty is just, I find the idea of deliberately planning to end someone's life nauseating. I remember reading the newspaper the morning after Saddam Hussein's execution by hanging in Iraq. It contained a photo of him the moment before the trapdoor opened and his life ended. In the article was a graphic description of the events that followed. Video footage from a mobile phone had ensured that the events would be available for the world to see. I didn't feel like eating breakfast that morning.

Yet when I read about the execution of Jesus, despite its being far more horrific, I find that it doesn't affect me in the same way. The differences of course are marked. Saddam was an evil man who deserved punishment; Jesus was a good man who did not deserve what he suffered. Saddam's death was quick and relatively painless; Jesus' death was publicly humiliating and agonizingly painful. Why is it that we can think about it without being moved? Perhaps we have become immune to the horror.

The cross has become the universal symbol of Christianity, yet in the first century it was not even mentioned in polite company. Mel Gibson's film *The Passion of the Christ* aroused debate because of its gruesome content. Yet the cross was a barbaric form of execution, deliberately designed to cause the most horrific physical suffering for as long as possible.

Yet, according to the Bible, it was not just the physical suffering that made the cross such an awful prospect for Jesus. In fact none of the Bible authors explain the crucifixion itself in much detail, focusing instead on a deeper aspect of Jesus' suffering.

During the crucifixion there were three hours of total darkness. In the Bible, darkness is a sign of God's anger. As Jesus dies, God's anger is being expressed in a very visual way. Jesus cries out, 'My God, my God, why have you forsaken me?'[2] God's anger is being directed towards Jesus. The one who had enjoyed an eternal relationship with his own Father is being separated from him. Worse than that: he is experiencing the anger of a holy God at the sin of the world. God's anger at murder, rape and child abuse, as well as at selfishness, dishonesty and gossip, was being poured out on Jesus. The unbearable consequences of evil were being experienced by Jesus on the cross.

A central message

This concept of Jesus taking the punishment for our sin is, as we've seen already, central to the whole message of the Bible. Before Jesus was even born, this event was expected and predicted. Seven hundred years earlier, his death had been described in vivid detail, and the reason for it explained. One of the Old Testament prophets, Isaiah, wrote: 'The punishment that brought us peace was upon him.'[3]

The New Testament part of the Bible looks back and explains this event. It is a common theme in every book. The apostle Paul talks about 'boast[ing] . . . in the cross'.[4] Peter explains that as Jesus died, 'He himself bore our sins in his body on the tree [another way of referring to the cross]'.[5]

Down through history, Christians have celebrated and sung about the cross. It has been not only the symbol of the faith, but the centre of its teaching. Christians sing about, mediate on and rejoice in the cross. This is reflected in the fact that Jesus' death is remembered annually on Good Friday.

Wonderful or wicked?

Yet why should such a horrific event be the foundation upon which Christianity is built? How can the day of Jesus' death be described as good? It is because in the terrible events of the cross something wonderful was being accomplished: our forgiveness and reconciliation with God.

Not everyone, however, looks on the cross in the same way. While it is celebrated and remembered by Christians around the world and through history, others object to it and find the whole concept horrific. For instance, Richard Dawkins says:

> I have described the atonement [the theological term to describe what happened on the cross], the central doctrine of Christianity as vicious, sadomasochistic and repellent. We should also dismiss it is as barking mad, but for its ubiquitous [ever-present] familiarity with which it has dulled our objectivity. If God wanted to forgive our sins, why not just forgive them, without having himself tortured and executed in payment?[6]

Christopher Hitchens agrees when he sarcastically observes, 'We have a father demonstrating his love by subjecting a son to death by torture.'[7]

Yet it is not only atheists who react against this view of Jesus' death. The Revd Jeffrey John, a Church of England cleric, said:

> What kind of God was this getting so angry with the world and the people he created, and then to calm himself down demanding the blood of his own son? And, anyway, why should God forgive us through punishing someone else?
> It is worse than illogical, it is insane. It made God sound like a psychopath. If any human being behaved like this we'd say they were a monster.[8]

These accusations are serious attacks at the very foundation of the Bible's message.

Misleading illustrations

One of the reasons why people have objected to the cross is because of the ways in which it has sometimes been explained. Christian speakers have often used illustrations to help explain why Jesus died. Some illuminate the truth in a very clear way, but others can be less helpful and actually contribute to this morally dubious view of God.

One frequently used story is of a group of prisoners of war who are lined up and accused of stealing a shovel (which in fact has not been stolen at all). They are told that unless someone owns up to the crime, they will all die. Eventually one prisoner steps forward to take responsibility, and as a result is bludgeoned to death. He was innocent, yet he died to save the others.

The problem with this story is that, taken to its logical conclusion, it portrays God as an irate camp commander punishing an innocent person for a crime that has not even been committed. The incident didn't need to happen and it shouldn't have happened.

Another illustration speaks of a father who operates a railway drawbridge. He is about to lower the bridge for the approaching train, when he sees his own son playing on the machinery below. If he lowers the bridge, his son will be crushed to death. If he doesn't, then hundreds of passengers will plunge to their deaths. At the last moment he lowers the bridge. His own son dies, but many passengers are saved.

This again can lead to a horrific view of God: a God who deliberately sends his Son to his death against his will, to save other people. What kind of God would treat his own Son like that?

Vicious?

It may appear to some that the cross is child abuse of the most vicious form. However, child abuse occurs when a child suffers against their will, or is not mature enough to make reasoned and responsible choices. Neither alternative applies in this situation.

Jesus spoke in a way that revealed that he knowingly and willingly went to the cross. The cross was as much his choice as it was the Father's plan. He said, 'No-one takes it [my life] from me, but I lay it down of my own accord. I have authority to lay it down and authority to take it up again.'[9] There is no disunity between God the Father's plan and God the Son's will. God was not punishing his Son against his will. The cross was not child abuse. Jesus knew and fully understood what would happen to him and died willingly. It was not that Jesus enjoyed the prospect of the cross. The Bible explains it was not the joy of his death, but of what his death would achieve, that motivated Jesus to do what he did. It says: 'For the joy set before him [he] endured the cross, scorning its shame, and sat down at the right hand of the throne of God.'[10]

Sadomasochistic?

Yet, even if Jesus willingly died, what kind of loving father would want to punish his own son in that way? Christians sometimes speak of the 'wrath of God being satisfied'. This seems to give the impression that God the Father got emotional satisfaction from punishing his own Son. The Bible is clear that it was God's plan for Jesus to die. One of the best-known verses in the Bible, quoted in the previous chapter, contains the words

The Bible is clear that it was God's plan for Jesus to die.

'God so loved the world that he gave his Son'.[11] Another verse goes as far as to say that it was 'the Lord's will to crush him and cause him to suffer'.[12]

But while it is clear that God was angry with Jesus on the cross, we shouldn't think that it was in some personal way. Jesus had done nothing to make God angry. It was the rest of humanity, ourselves included, who deserved to face God's anger. Yet, as Jesus died, he took upon himself the evil of the world and, in doing so, the anger of God at all of it. Jesus willingly stepped into our shoes and took upon himself what we deserved.

God's anger does not contradict his love. It is because God loves that he gets angry. If I love someone, then I will be rightly angry when someone else hurts that person. Not to be angry would actually show that I didn't really love them. In the same way, God is angry at the people who hurt us because he loves us. This also means that he is angry at us when, through our own selfishness, we hurt other people.

We should be the ones who experience God's anger. The wonder is that when Jesus died, he took what we deserved. God did not get joy from doing it. 'Satisfaction' does not refer to God gaining pleasure from Jesus' death, but rather that God's wrath was fully spent or exhausted, and the requirements of his justice and law had been met. The full extent of God's rightful anger at sin was taken by Jesus, so that it doesn't have to fall on us.

Another reason to dismiss the 'sadomasochistic' claim is that God was not inflicting pain on someone else at the cross. It was not a third party who was suffering but God himself, because the Son and the Father are not two separate gods, but one. The Bible declares that there is one God, but he has revealed himself in three persons: Father, Son and Spirit. Some find this concept (often referred to as 'the Trinity') a stumbling-block, but it doesn't need to be. A God who is big enough to create the universe *should* be – at least in some ways – totally beyond our comprehension![13]

However, while this is not simple to understand, its implications are important, especially in relation to the cross. The fact that there is one God, not three, affects the way we look at Jesus' death. At the cross, God was not punishing a third party but actually dealing with the consequences of our sin within himself.

A father disciplining a son may be heard to say, 'This hurts me as much as it hurts you.' I remember that, as a child, I put a plastic plate down my trousers before I was smacked, so for once that statement proved true!

At the cross, God experienced pain within his own being. He took upon himself the pain of making possible our forgiveness. It is amazing to think that God himself was willing to suffer for us.

Repellent?

But, you may be asking, why did God have to suffer at all? Couldn't he simply forgive us, without this repellent talk of blood and death?

Yet when it comes to forgiveness, does anyone *just* forgive? Someone I know witnessed his friend being killed by a drunk driver. How would he react if I said to him, 'Well, just forgive him'? It is not that forgiveness is impossible, but neither is it easy. No one *just* forgives. It is always painful.

Our natural reaction to evil is to want to get even. We want to repay the other person with the pain that we have experienced. When we forgive, we choose not to get even or repay; rather, we experience the pain ourselves. The greater the crime committed, the more painful the forgiveness. In the cross we see a cosmic version of this being played out. Rather than getting even, God himself experiences the pain of our sin so we can experience forgiveness.

Forgiveness is not easy; it is painful. Nor is it cheap, but costly. If I lend my car to a friend and he crashes it as a result of bad driving, I can choose to forgive him. However, I cannot then send him the bill for getting it fixed! In forgiving, I choose to take upon myself the cost of sorting out the problem.

At the cross, we see that God took upon himself the cost and the pain of our forgiveness. Our sin and rebellion against God has consequences and must be paid for. But Jesus paid the price.

Bear in mind the end of the story

I got into Harry Potter a bit later than the rest of the world. When most people had finished Book Seven, I was only just starting Book One. The danger of reading it when I did was that people could very easily let slip what happened later in the series. That's exactly what happened a few weeks later, as I was chatting to a friend. Presuming that I was reading the last book, he let slip a highly significant event that came at the end of the penultimate one. I was really upset, but to his credit he did apologize and even bought me the book as a present.

Knowing the information I did caused me to come to certain conclusions about the characters in the book. Some I saw in a whole new light. But when I eventually came to the end of the final book, I had a shock. I realized that some of my conclusions had been wrong. I hadn't heard the whole story. Only at the end of the last book was I in a position to make a correct judgment.

Looking at the cross out of context may cause us to come to all kinds of wrong conclusions about God's character. The cross is the centre of the story, but it is certainly not the end. Jesus willingly went through it because he knew what it would achieve. The Bible gives us a glimpse of the end of the story. It shows that the cross brought about the rescue of millions of people from all over the world and throughout history. These people enjoy a renewed world in all its glory, with Jesus, the true and rightful king of it all, at the centre. Nothing is there to spoil it. Death will never end it. It is a wonderful hope that can be ours because of the cross.

Destroying our only hope

A doctor in America was called out in the middle of the night to operate on a girl who had been involved in a serious accident. He got up as quickly as he could and jumped into his car to drive to the hospital. On the way he had to stop at some traffc lights. As he waited for them to turn green, a brick came smashing through the window. Moments later he was being pulled out of the car. He was left at the side of the road as his attacker drove off.

Getting up from the ground, he eventually managed to find a taxi and reach the hospital, but the delay had been too long. The child had died. He was asked if he would go and break the news to the parents. Stepping out into the waiting area, the doctor saw the couple he was about to speak to. Suddenly he noticed that the father looked familiar. It was the same man who had stolen his car. In his desperation to get to the hospital himself, the man had destroyed his only hope. He had rejected the person who was able to save his daughter.

If we reject the cross, we reject our only hope. It is only the cross that deals with the heart of the human problem. Only in Jesus' death do we find the possibility of real forgiveness and reconciliation with God. God is not vicious or sado-masochistic, and his ways are not repellent. The cross reveals his infinite love and wisdom. We reject the cross at our own expense.

11. AWESOME, LOVING AND AMAZINGLY GRACIOUS

What kind of person would reject a God so good?

It was election time and, as I drove down the road, a large billboard grabbed my attention. Displayed across it was the face of a well-known political leader. At first I thought it was advertising the leader's own political party. I soon noticed, however, that the photo had been changed. It now showed demonic eyes and devil's horns. It was a smear campaign by the opposition.

In politics, smear campaigns can be very successful. Instead of objective discussion of the facts, we find character assassination being attempted. Details of drug experimentation in a politician's teenage years are leaked to the press. Of course, sometimes such campaigns can backfire. When they do, they often reveal more about the character of the person who initiated the campaign than the person smeared.

Could it be that through history there has been a subtle, yet even more successful smear campaign? Only this isn't against a politician or celebrity, but against God himself. Have you ever wondered why Christianity is so often sidelined in the public arena? Why it is that in the media Christians are often ridiculed and mocked? What it is that makes atheists like Richard Dawkins so passionate in their rejection of a God they don't even believe exists? Why the Bible has been the subject of more critical debate than any other book in history, yet is still read and believed by millions?

In my experience, most people have not rejected Christianity because the evidence has persuaded them that it is not true. Most have not even looked into the evidence. I remember speaking at a pudding night at a university. Afterwards, I got chatting to a lad as we tucked into our third helping of lemon meringue pie. We had a great chat, as he fired what seemed like 101 questions at me. Before we finished, I had one question for him: 'If I could answer all your questions satisfactorily,' I asked, 'would you become a Christian?' He thought for a moment and then quite confidently replied, 'No.'

As we continued to talk, his real problem with God became clear. Whether Christianity was true or not wasn't the issue. Even if it was, he still would not believe. His real issue was that it just didn't seem good. He didn't want to trust in a God who seemed so outdated, repressive and boring. He felt he was better off without him. But how did he come to that conclusion? Had God's character been smeared?

A global smear campaign

Close to the start of the book of Genesis, we read about the very first smear campaign in human history. Behind it stands Satan himself. In attempting to get people to turn away from God, his tactic is not to deny God's existence. Much more subtly, he calls God's goodness into question. By giving the impression that God is withholding good things from them, he could cause humanity to reject God and in doing so ruin the world. His tactics were successful. As we have already seen, the consequences of that initial act of rebellion have affected the world ever since.

Satan's tactics haven't changed. He knows that to get us to reject God, he doesn't need to make us deny his existence. Deep down, we have a sneaking suspicion that he is there anyway. But if we doubt his goodness, then we can happily go our own way. Not only that, but we will tell ourselves that we are liberated, free and able to enjoy life more fully.

As we move through the story of the Old Testament, we see how the smear campaign continues. God calls out a special people to be his own. He rescues them from slavery and is leading them to a land that will be their own. Along the way, he miraculously protects and cares for them on a daily basis. Yet after all the evidence of God's goodness, they rebel against God. They conclude: 'The Lord hates us; so he brought us out of Egypt to . . . destroy us.'[1] They seem blind to all the evidence of God's goodness. The consequences of their rebellion are disastrous.

The campaign is still there in the New Testament. On one occasion Jesus miraculously heals a man of blindness.[2] Yet despite seeing this wonderful act of compassion, the religious leaders are outraged. How dare Jesus do such a thing on the Jewish holy day? Jesus points out the irony of the situation. The blind man can now see, but those who claim to see are in fact blind. They rub shoulders daily with the best man who ever lived, and yet they end up planning to kill him.

Satan's tactics are the same today. The Bible says, 'The god of this age [one of the Bible's descriptions of Satan] has blinded the minds of unbelievers, so that they cannot see the light of the gospel of the glory of Christ, who is the image of God.'[3] We have been blinded to God's goodness in Jesus.

For a smear campaign, subtlety works best. So Jesus isn't always derided. Rather, he is dismissed as unimportant and irrelevant. Christians are mocked as being outdated. God is blamed for not stopping suffering and environmental disasters. Churches are reported only when they face problems and splits. Religion is seen as the source of all violence. The amazing way of getting right with God is viewed as petty and exclusive. God's justice is made to appear unjust. The cross of Jesus is dismissed as weak and foolish.

Starting to see

As a child I used to love watching at TV show called *Cartoon Time*. In part of the show the host would draw a well-known cartoon character, and as he did so, he would keep asking the audience the same question: 'Can you tell what it is yet?' For a while it didn't seem to resemble anything: just a random collection of lines and scribbles. Then, slowly, features would appear: a mouth – an ear – a pair of eyes – and suddenly it would all become clear.

As you have read through this book, I hope you may have started to see more clearly the kind of God who is revealed in the Bible. Perhaps you have begun to see that, when they are thought through, the accusations don't stand up in the way you thought they did before. God is not the evil tyrant that some would have us believe. Actually, he is amazingly good and totally trustworthy.

We have seen that, rather than being distant and uninterested, God has clearly revealed himself to us. Not only through the creation around us and our conscience within us; God has shown himself most clearly through Jesus. The claims Jesus made are so huge that we cannot say they are irrelevant. They affect every human being alive in the universe.

Nor is God apathetic to the problems of our world. Suffering is real and it hurts, but we have seen that it is not God's fault. God has not only experienced suffering himself on the cross, but he has done something about it. Even the physical world we live in matters to God. He wants us to look after it and has given the amazing hope that one day it will be renewed and made perfect. All that spoils this world will be taken away.

Sadly, war, violence and hypocrisy are daily realities in our world. Sometimes those who have claimed to follow God have been to blame. However, we have seen that in the course of history God has often been misrepresented by those who profess to follow him. They have been inconsistent with Jesus and have misinterpreted the Bible. The true followers of Jesus are those who take seriously his command to love their enemies. Consistent Christianity will have a positive impact on society, as it has done in the past. While some churches have moved away from Jesus' teaching, authentic Christian communities are brilliant places to be. The Christian message sets people free from judgmental attitudes and allows people to be accepted as they are.

To many, Christianity may seem petty and exclusive. Yet we have seen that, in his wisdom, God has created a way by which he has made it possible for people to be brought into relationship with him. We should not complain that there is only *one* way, but be thankful that there is *a* way. The offer of forgiveness and acceptance is available not just to some, but to all who will trust Jesus. His way of living is not restrictive and repressive. Even the Bible's blueprint for sex is for our good. Living God's way means living in the way we were created to do, experiencing solid joy and lasting pleasure.

When we think about hell, it may appear that God is arbitrary and unjust. Yet it is because of his goodness that he has set a date when justice will be done. Every wrong will be put right, because God cares deeply about us. Even though his judgment has serious consequences for us, because of our rebellion, he has provided a way to be rescued from it. His death on the cross took the punishment that our rebellion deserved. Jesus' willing sacrifice makes it possible for us to be forgiven and brought into a relationship with God.

Be suspicious of your suspicions

It may well be, though, that you are still not convinced. In fact, you may have thought up more questions while you have been reading the answers to these. You feel you still have enough reasons to stop you having to make any big changes in your thinking. If that's what you're feeling, it's good to remember that when it comes to the question of God, none of us are objective. Not only have we been influenced by Satan's smear campaign, but our own hearts are biased. When we are making up our minds, we are influenced not only by what *seems* to be true but also what we *want* to be true.

> *When we are making up our minds, we are influenced not only by what seems to be true but also what we want to be true.*

One evening I was driving across town to meet some friends. As I approached a set of traffc lights, they began to change. I nipped through before they turned to red – or so I thought. A few moments later I saw blue flashing lights in my rear-view mirror. I pulled over at the side of the road, expecting whoever it was behind me to drive on past. To my surprise the driver also pulled up, right behind me. For some reason, I thought to myself that it was a real coincidence that they had stopped in the same place as I had! It was only when a uniformed man started walking towards my car that I started to realize something was wrong.

At that moment I had a choice. I could try and explain away what was happening to me, or I could face up to it. I could assume that the lights were not those of a police car, but only reflections off the surrounding buildings. The sound of the siren could actually have been my squeaky brakes. The person walking towards me was not a policeman, but just some guy in fancy dress. I could explain it away and drive off. But the truth would soon catch up with me – literally! Much better to face up to the situation. I didn't want it to be that way, but it was. (Thankfully, the policeman was in a good mood that day.)

It may be that, as you have read through the book, you have started to feel uncomfortable. What if this is true? We can always think of more excuses, which may satisfy us on the surface, but the nagging question remains. What if the God that I have rejected is not who I thought he was? What will that mean for me?

What if this is true?

Facing up to the truth

A friend told me about an embarrassing experience that he recently had while shopping. After buying a card, he thought that the shopkeeper had short-changed him. He thought he had given the shopkeeper a ten-pound note, but only received the change for five pounds. He was demanding that he should be given the rest of the change, when the man behind him in the queue pointed out that he had in fact only given £5 in the first place. He felt awful. It was not the shopkeeper who was at fault, but himself.

One of the reasons why we don't want to face up to the goodness of God is that it changes the way we view ourselves. The kind of God that Richard Dawkins describes can make us feel quite good about ourselves. By comparison with that kind of God, we are nice, respectable and caring people. It is he who is in the wrong, not us. But what if in fact it is the other way round? What if it is God who is good and we who are not?

The consequences of rejecting that kind of God would be pretty serious. We would have spent our lives rejecting the good and loving Creator of the universe. We would have lived in his world and yet ignored him.

A friend of mine flies aeroplanes. He tells me that if you think you have a problem with a plane, then the one thing you don't do is ignore it! That would also be good advice here. Don't just choose to ignore what we have seen to be true about God, and hope that it will go away. Do something about it.

So what would be a good way to respond?

Turn

Jesus says that the right way to respond to God is to 'repent and believe'.[4] To repent is to turn around. It is what my Sat-Nav tells me to do, every time I forget to take the right road while I'm driving. In our thinking about God we need a huge turnaround. No longer am I at the centre, with God on the outside. Nor am I the good one sitting in judgment on God. From now on, he takes centre stage. His way is good, and I put an end to my independence. My life is going to be lived his way.

I remember talking to a student in a Christian Union. A year previously, he had come to some of the Christian Union events. He was an atheist and keen for a good debate.

Convinced that he could prove them wrong, he enjoyed the discussions with the Christians after the meetings. But the more he questioned, the more he began to doubt his doubts. Eventually, he faced up to what he had been aware of for a while, but had been unwilling to admit: God was not only real but also good. But how can God accept someone like him?

Trust

The Bible says that, even while we were still independently living our own way, God was making it possible for us to come back to him. In the book of Romans we are told: 'God demonstrates his own love for us in this: While we were still sinners, Christ died for us.'[5] It is an incredible thing that, before we even thought about God, he had already thought about us. Before we even considered turning to him, he was making it possible for us to be forgiven.

When Jesus died, he took the punishment for all our rebellion and rejection of him. He dealt with our problem and made it possible for us to be brought back into a relationship with God. The right response to this is to believe. Believing is not an irrational thing done by weird and religious people. It is something we do, in different ways, every day. It means trusting in something we are persuaded is trustworthy.

Jesus says that we should believe in him. When we do, we receive his forgiveness and are accepted by God. Only his work is suffcient to deal with the size of our need. We are rebels who need rescuing. Jesus came to achieve that rescue for us.

What kind of God?

We have seen that, contrary to popular opinion, the God of the Bible is not only real but totally good. He is both clear and relevant. He cares about his world and understands the suffering of people within it. He is utterly consistent and amazingly patient. In his wisdom and care, he has revealed the best way to live. He is compassionate, life-giving, merciful and loving. What will your response be? Will you succumb to Satan's smear campaign and the bias of your own heart? Or will you face up to the truth about him and trust him for yourself?

12. OVER TO YOU NOW

Could it be that you now realize that you need to do something about what you now know? You don't necessarily have all the answers to your questions, but what you know has persuaded you. You realize that it is reasonable to believe that God is both good and trustworthy. Right now, you could do something about it. A great place to start would be to talk to God. Tell him that you are sorry for the way you have treated him. Ask him to forgive you and accept you on the basis of what Jesus has done. Decide that from now on you want to live with him at the centre of your life.

If this is something you know you need to do, the following prayer might be helpful. It's like one that I prayed when I first put my trust in Jesus. It's not a magical formula, but it is a way of expressing to God what we have been thinking about. Why not read it and think it through? If it would be a good prayer for you, then say it to God, either out loud or in your mind.

Heavenly Father,

I am sorry for the way that I have rejected you. Sorry for the things that I have done that have shown that I have lived my own way and not yours. Thank you so much that in your love you planned to rescue me from my rebellion. Thank you that Jesus willingly died so that I could be forgiven. Please forgive me and help me from now on to live your way, with you at the centre of my life.

Amen

What if you didn't?

It may be that you didn't feel ready yet to take that step. I hope, though, that it has at least become clear that it is really important. The issues at stake are of eternal importance. It would be great to find a place where you can look more closely at what God is like and keep asking questions. Go to www.alpha.org or www.christianityexplored.org to find details of a great course in your area, where you can do this.

What if you did?

However, if you did pray that prayer, then congratulations! Putting our trust in Jesus is the most important and best decision we can make. You may be wondering where you go from here.

Go public

Throughout this book we have discovered that Christianity is not just a private belief or an interesting philosophy. It is public truth about a real God who has made himself known. So part of being a Christian means being open about our trust in him. Once we have discovered the truth about God and his goodness, then it is right that we want to help other people see that too. It won't be easy. Satan's smear campaign has been very successful. Remember, it worked on us for a while. However, God can use us to help people come to discover the truth about him.[1]

Grow the relationship

We have already seen something of God's amazing goodness. Living as a Christian means beginning a journey where we discover more and more about this God. It is a relationship that should get deeper as our understanding of him gets better.

Many people's ideas about God have been based more on their feelings than on objective truth. If we are going to get to know God better, we will need to make sure that we don't rely only on our emotions. We need to get stuck into the Bible, where we can objectively understand more about God as he reveals himself to us. As we do so, our relationship grows deeper.

We can also to talk to God. As we pray, we speak to him as we would speak to a friend. You don't need to use set words or phrases. We can thank him for the things that we are discovering about him and ask for help to live his way. Because he is good, we can trust him with things that trouble us, knowing that he cares.

Don't go it alone

God has set up the church, an amazing community of people who have come to discover his goodness and trust him. His plan for you is to be a part of it too. As someone who has come into relationship with him, you are already a part of this global community. It is most likely that there will be a local expression of it that meets somewhere near you. Look for one where their views about God are shaped by what the Bible says, and where they talk a lot about Jesus.

Enjoy
Being a Christian means living life in the way it was meant to be lived, with God at the centre. It isn't about missing out on life, but discovering it in all its fullness. That doesn't mean it is always going to be easy. Often it will mean going against the flow of the society around you. But it is worth it. God is good, and we can trust him.

If you would like to ask me any questions, then please don't hesitate to get in touch. Go to www.moetonline.org

FURTHER READING

1: Distant, uninterested and silent?

Michael Ots, *But Is It True?* (London, IVP, 2016): a look at the evidence for the Christian faith.

Lee Strobel, *The Case for Christ* (Grand Rapids (MI), Zondervan, 1998): a sceptic's search through the historical evidence for Jesus.

James Sire, *Why Should Anyone Believe Anything at All?* (Downers Grove (IL), IVP, 1994): looking at the basis of belief and the evidence for Christianity.

Amy Orr-Ewing, *Why Trust the Bible?* (Leicester, IVP, 2005): really helpful answers to some of the biggest questions about the Bible.

John Dickson, *If I was God I'd Make Myself Clearer* (New Malden, Matthias Media, 2000): a short book explaining how God has revealed himself.

Rodney Holder, *Big Bang, Big God: A Universe Designed for Life?* (Oxford, Lion Books, 2013): a look at how scientific evidence for the beginning and the fine tuning of the universe points us towards God as the most reasonable explanation.

2: Outdated, out of touch and old-fashioned?

Mike Cain, *Real Life Jesus* (Nottingham, IVP, 2008): looks at the relevance of Jesus' life and claims, as found in John's Gospel.

Michael Green, *Jesus for Sceptics* (Oxford, UCCF, 2013): a helpful guide into looking at the evidence for Jesus.

Tom Wright, *The Original Jesus: The Life and Vision of a Revolutionary* (Grand Rapids, Eerdmans, 1997): a brilliant introduction on the relevance of Jesus Christ for everyone.

3: Rape, child abuse and Aids

Sharon Dirckx, *Why?* (Nottingham, IVP, 2013): a helpful introduction to a very difficult subject.

Ravi Zacharias and Vince Vitale, *Why Suffering?* (FaithWords, 2014): looks at suffering from both the philosophical and the personal perspective.

Pablo Martinez, *A Thorn in the Flesh* (Nottingham, IVP, 2007): examines how God can use for good the suffering in our lives.

4: Carbon footprints, global warming and climate change

Dave Bookless, *Planetwise* (Nottingham, IVP, 2008): shows clearly what the Bible has to say about our attitude to the environment, with practical suggestions of what we can do.

Julian Hardyman, *Glory Days* (Nottingham, IVP, 2006): shows how God is interested in every part of our lives – including our attitude to the environment.

A Rocha (website: www.arocha.org) is a Christian nature conservation organization.

5: Crusades, inquisitions and car bombs

Rodney Stark, *For the Glory of God* (Princeton (NJ), Princeton University Press, 2004): a sociologist looks at the influence of Christianity during the course of history.

Nick Solly Megoran, *The War on Terror* (Nottingham, IVP, 2007): a Christian response to the problem of terrorism.

Alister E. McGrath with Joanna C. McGrath, *The Dawkins Delusion?* (London, SPCK, 2007): a reasoned and level-headed response to the accusations made by Richard Dawkins, including the claim that religion causes violence.

Paul Copan, *Is God a Moral Monster?* (Grand Rapids, Baker, 2011): a response to the moral objections to the God of the Old Testament.

6: Hypocritical, divided and judgmental?

Joshua Harris, *Stop Dating the Church* (Sisters (OR), Multnomah, 2004): shows why God thinks so much of the church, and why we should be a part of it.

Graham Beynon, *God's New Community* (Leicester, IVP, 2005): a really clear and helpful look at what the New Testament teaches about the church.

7: Petty, intolerant and exclusive?

Ravi Zacharias, *Jesus among Other Gods: The Absolute Claims of the Christian Message* (Nashville, Thomas Nelson, 2010): a helpful comparison of Jesus and other world faiths.

Michael Green, *But Don't All Religions Lead to God?* (Nashville, Thomas Nelson, 2010): unpacks the common idea that all religions are basically the same and looks at the unique claims of Jesus.

Chris Wright, *The Uniqueness of Jesus* (*Thinking Clearly Series*) (London, Monarch, 2001): shows how Jesus is different from all other figures of history.

Malcolm Steer, *A Muslim's Pocket Guide to Christianity* (Fearn, Christian Focus, 2005): a helpful handbook for Muslims wanting to understand Christianity.

8: Repressive, restrictive and restraining?

Linda Marshall, *Pure* (Leicester, IVP, 2005): a short book looking at the Bible's teaching on sex and relationships.

Nigel Pollock, *Relationships Revolution* (Leicester, IVP, 1998): a general book about relationships.

Ed Shaw, *The Plausibility Problem* (Nottingham, IVP: 2015): a look at what the Bible says about same-sex attraction from someone for whom this is personally a real issue.

9: Condemning, unjust and arbitrary?

Dick Dowsett, *God, That's Not Fair* (Milton Keynes, Authentic, 2006): looks at how to reconcile the Bible's teaching on hell with God's justice and goodness.

C. S. Lewis, *The Great Divorce* (London, Fount, 2002): a short, thought-provoking book about heaven and hell.

10: 'Vicious, sadomasochistic and repellent'?

Mark Meynell, *Cross Examined* (Leicester, IVP, 2005): a clear explanation of the significance of the death of Jesus.

John Stott, *The Cross of Christ* (Nottingham, IVP, 2006): A more in-depth examination of the subject.

Books that look at a number of related issues:

John Lennox, *Gunning for God* (Oxford, Lion, 2011): tackles a number of the main objections that are raised by new atheists.

Timothy Keller, *The Reason for God* (London, Hodder and Stoughton, 2009): looks at many of the main objections people have to the Christian faith and explains the heart of the Christian message.

Alister E. McGrath with Joanna C. McGrath, *The Dawkins Delusion?* (London, SPCK, 2007): a reasoned and level-headed response to the accusations made by Richard Dawkins.

Philip J. Sampson, *Six Modern Myths about Christianity and Western Civilization* (Leicester, IVP, 2000): unpacking myths about Christianity.

Nicky Gumbel, *Searching Issues* (Eastbourne, Kingsway, 2004): simple answers to seven of the most common questions asked about Christianity.

Vincent Carroll and David Shiflett, *Christianity on Trial* (New York, Encounter, 2001): answers some of the popular accusations against Christianity.

Peter Meadows and Joseph Steinberg, *Beyond Belief* (Milton Keynes, Authentic, 1999): written in a very engaging and refreshing way, this simple book explains the basics of Christian belief while taking into account people's objections to it.

www.bethinking.org – a really helpful website for people wanting to think through the big questions about life, the universe and God. Loads of helpful resources to read or listen to.

Books that look more closely at Jesus and what it means to follow him:

Mike Cain, *Real Life Jesus* (Nottingham, IVP, 2008): explains Jesus' life and claims as found in John's Gospel and shows how they affect us today.

John Stott, *Basic Christianity* (Nottingham, IVP, 2008): a classic
book introducing people to the basics of Christianity.

John Chapman, *A Fresh Start* (New Malden, The Good Book
Company, 1997): shows what it means to be a Christian,
and how to become one.

Books for those starting out as Christians:

Nicky Gumbel, *A Life Worth Living* (Eastbourne, Kingsway,
2001): a study guide, written for new Christians, that
takes you through the New Testament book of
Philippians.

John White, *The Fight* (Leicester, IVP, 2002): a practical
handbook for Christian living.

Nigel Beynon and Andrew Sach, *Dig Deeper* (Leicester, IVP,
2005): a toolkit that helps you start studying the Bible for
yourself.

Courses where you can find out more:

Christianity Explored (www.christianityexplored.org) takes
you through Mark's Gospel and introduces you to Jesus.
After a talk or video, there is time for group study and
discussion.

Alpha (www.alpha.org) gives you the opportunity to
explore the meaning of life and discover more about the
Christian faith.

To find details of a course being held near you, have a look
at the website.

Finding your way around the Bible

The Bible is split up in various ways. First, it is divided into
two main parts. The Old Testament contains books written
before Jesus' birth, while the New Testament contains
books written during the first century. Each main part is

then divided into different books: thirty-nine of them in the
Old Testament and twenty-seven in the New. The name of
each book either refers to its author, or is a brief description
of its contents. The Bible contains different types of
literature: history, poetry, prophecy, and so on. Most of the
quotations in this book come from the Gospels – first-
century accounts of Jesus' life and work.

Each book is divided into chapters and verses. The original
authors didn't do this; these divisions were added later, to
help us make sure we were all looking at the same part of
the same book. Chapters are the large numbers dividing the
text, and verses are the smaller numbers inserted in the text
itself. So 'John 3:16' means that you'll find the quotation in
the book called John, at chapter 3 and verse 16.

NOTES

Introduction

1. R. Dawkins, *The God Delusion* (London, Bantam, 2006), p. 31.
2. C. Hitchens, *God is Not Great* (London, Atlantic, 2007), from the cover.
3. From the Frank Zappa album, *You Are What You Is*, © 1981 Munchkin Music. All rights reserved. Used by permission.

Chapter 1: Distant, uninterested and silent?

1. R. Dawkins, *The God Delusion*, p. 50.
2. C. Hitchens, *God is Not Great*, p. 282.
3. Romans 1:20.
4. James Sire, *Why Should Anyone Believe Anything at All?* (Downers Grove (IL), IVP, 1994), p. 171.
5. John 1:1.
6. John 1:14.
7. R. Dawkins, *The God Delusion*, p. 97.
8. Hebrews 1:1.
9. If you would like to receive a copy of Mark's Gospel, then please contact me with your name and postal address at moetonline.org, and I will gladly send you one.

Chapter 2: Outdated, out of touch and old-fashioned?

1. Luke 4:18–19.
2. Luke 4:21.
3. John 8:53.
4. John 8:58.
5. John 14:6.
6. John 14:9.
7. John 11:25.
8. Matthew 28:19–20.
9. John 3:14–15.
10. C. S. Lewis, *God in the Dock* (Grand Rapids (MI), Eerdmans, 1994 [originally published 1952, from radio talks given by C. S. Lewis in 1942–4]).
11. R. Dawkins, *The God Delusion*, p. 92.
12. John 3:16–17.

Chapter 3: Rape, child abuse and Aids

1. Assuming it takes twenty minutes to read a chapter, and using current statistics from the World Health Organization and the United Nations.
2. It is estimated that around 200 million people, or 5,479 people per day, died during the twentieth century through wars, conflicts, massacres and oppression (http:users.erols.com/ mwhite28/warstat8.htm). In the terrorist attacks in the USA on 11 September 2001, 2,998 people died (http://en.wikipedia.org/ wiki/September_11,_2001_attacks).
3. Richard Dawkins, *River out of Eden: A Darwinian View of Life* (London, Phoenix, 1995), p. 133.
4. Genesis 1:31.
5. Romans 8:20, 22.
6. Mark 7:21–22.
7. Luke 13:2–3a.
8. Luke 13:3b.

9. 2 Peter 3:9b.

10. John Stott, *The Cross of Christ* (Nottingham, IVP, 2006), pp. 335–336.

11. James Sire, *Why Should Anyone Believe Anything at All?*, p. 188.

12. Romans 8:32.

13. Revelation 21:1–5.

14. Romans 8:18.

Chapter 4: Carbon footprints, global warming and climate change

1. http://www.ft.com/cms/s/0/c24ba6c2-8f99-11e5-a549-b89a1dfede9b.html#axzz3sVJndX7A http://ocean.nationalgeographic.com/ocean/critical-issues-sea-level-rise/

2. http://www.economist.com/news/economic-and-financial-indicators/21657796-global-threats

3. http://www.bbc.co.uk/news/business-34396961

4. http://cotap.org/per-capita-carbon-co2-emissions-by-country/?gclid=CjwKEAjwnf2wBRCf3sOp6oTtnjYSJAANOfheG8_ZO-ILzzOjJ-Y2H1OcGHRgoerBlN-LYXr-wLO5oRoCu6zw_wcB

5. As quoted by R. Dawkins, *The God Delusion*, p. 288.

6. Genesis 1.

7. Romans 8:21.

8. John 1:14.

9. 1 John 1:1.

10. This concept comes from John Stott, *Issues Facing Christians Today* (London, Marshall Pickering, 1990), p. 117.

11. Psalm 24:1.

12. Psalm 115:16.

13. Revelation 14:13.

Chapter 5: Crusades, inquisitions and car bombs

1. C. Hitchens, *God is Not Great*, p. 25.

2. R. Dawkins, *The God Delusion*, pp. 1, 2.

3. From Pascal's *Pensées*.
4. Alister E. McGrath with Joanna C. McGrath, *The Dawkins Delusion?* (London, SPCK, 2007), p. 50.
5. John 4:21, 23.
6. See Mark 8:27–33.
7. See Ephesians 6:10–18.
8. For some examples, see John Pollock, *A Fistful of Heroes: Great Reformers and Evangelists* (Basingstoke, Marshall Pickering, 1988).
9. Luke 9:51–56.
10. Matthew 5:9, 44.
11. Luke 23:34.
12. See Mark 7:20–23.
13. Isaiah 2:4.

Chapter 6: Hypocritical, divided and judgmental

1. Ephesians 3:10.
2. Matthew 9:9–13.
3. Matthew 7:16–20.
4. Matthew 23.
5. 1 Corinthians 15:3.
6. Luke 18:9–14.

Chapter 7: Petty, intolerant and exclusive?

1. Genesis 1:31.
2. Revelation 21:1.
3. Revelation 21:4.
4. John 3:7.
5. Adapted from an illustration in Mike Cain, *Real Life Jesus* (Nottingham, IVP, 2008).
6. 2 Corinthians 5:17.
7. See http://news.bbc.co.uk/1/hi/uk_politics/6219626.stm
8. See http://news.bbc.co.uk/1/hi/uk/4125229.stm

9. Genesis 12:3.

10. Luke 2:10.

11. John 4:42.

12. Acts 1:8.

13. Revelation 7:9.

Chapter 8: Repressive, restrictive and restraining?

1. Quoted in Nicky Gumbel, *Searching Issues* (Eastbourne, Kingsway, 2004), p. 39.

2. Quoted in Nicky Gumbel, *Searching Issues*, p. 39.

3. Genesis 1:31.

4. 1 Corinthians 7:5.

5. Genesis 2:24.

6. Matthew 19:5.

7. Divorce is 60% more likely after eight years of marriage among couples who cohabited before marriage: statistics quoted in Nicky Gumbel, *Searching Issues*, p. 44.

8. http://health.discovery.com/centers/loverelationships/articles/marriage_myths.html; http://www.huffingtonpost.com/2012/04/13/marriage-sex_n_1422644.html

9. 1 Corinthians 6:18.

10. Romans 1:25.

11. See Ephesians 5:22–33.

12. John 17:3.

13. 1 John 1:9.

14. John 10:10.

Chapter 9: Condemning, unjust and arbitrary?

1. Luke 16:19–31.

2. Mark 9:48.

3. Matthew 8:12.

4. Matthew 25:41.

5. Romans 2:5.

6. Acts 17:31.

7. Ian Rankin, *The Times*, 20 November 2002.

8. Mark 7:20–23.

9. Psalm 51:4.

10. Luke 16:19–31.

11. 2 Peter 3:9.

12. John 3:16.

Chapter 10: 'Vicious, sadomasochistic and repellent'?

1. R. Dawkins, *The God Delusion*, p. 253.

2. Mark 15:34.

3. Isaiah 53:5.

4. Galatians 6:14.

5. 1 Peter 2:24.

6. R. Dawkins, *The God Delusion*, p. 253.

7. C. Hitchens, *God is Not Great*, p. 209.

8. http://www.telegraph.co.uk/news/main.jhtml?xml=/news/
2007/04/05/ndean05.xml

9. John 10:18.

10. Hebrews 12:2.

11. John 3:16.

12. Isaiah 53:10.

13. A helpful book for thinking more about the Trinity is Tim
Chester, *Delighting in the Trinity* (Oxford, Monarch Books, 2005).

Chapter 11: Awesome, loving and amazingly gracious

1. Deuteronomy 1:27.

2. John 9.

3. 2 Corinthians 4:4.

4. Mark 1:15.

5. Romans 5:8.

12: Over to you now

1. The thought of talking about God with others may fill some with dread. For a down-to-earth and helpful guide in knowing how to tell other people, read John Chapman, *Know and Tell the Gospel* (New Malden, The Good Book Company, 1998).